Bobby L. Woods

Marriages Are Made In Heaven

Copyright © 2021 by Bobby L. Woods. All rights reserved.

Bobby L. Woods

Not Just Alphabets Publishing

Las Vegas, Nevada

All Not Just Alphabets Publishing titles, Emanuel Cole, imprints and lines distributed are available at special quantity discounts for bulk purchases for sales promotion, fund raising, premiums, educational, institutional and library use.

Copyright © 2021 by Bobby L. Woods. All rights reserved.

No part of this work may be reproduced or transmitted in any form or by any means, electronic or mechanical, including photocopying and recording, or by any information storage retrieval system without the prior written permission of Bobby L. Woods, or Not Just Alphabets.
Email tommie0713@att.net address for Permission.

Printed in the U. S. A.

Library of Congress Catalog Card Number:

ISBN: 978 - 1 - 7338810 - 9 - 8

Bobby L. Woods

INTRODUCTION

Why I chose this title, "Marriages Are Made In Heaven". I truly believe that God designs a specific mate for those who are to be married. And He brings them together at His appointed time.

When I began pinning this book, I had been married fifty years to young girl I met in 1958. I was never able to get her out of my mind. I supposed one would say, "I fell in love when I saw her. She was 14 years old, I was 18 years old, so that was a no, no.

She graduated high school and moved to New York. I was drafted into the United State Army and was deployed to Germany. I didn't think we would ever be together.

In God's time He brought us together in an unusual way. After about nine years with little to no communication she got on my mind so intense, it was my birthday. September 1, 1967, I got her phone number from my sister and called her, I said, "I'm ready to get married, what about you?" She said, "Yes." Two weeks later she came to Dayton, OH, and on September 27, 1967 we exchanged marital vows and we are yet together. We've endued better or worse, richer or poorer, sickness and health but true love, which is God's love keeps us together.

I believe God ordained marriage for the purpose of companionship, procreation, and ministry according to Genesis 1:27 - 28. Genesis 2: 24 says, two (male & female) to become one flesh, only God can make / cause two (male & female) to become one flesh. He commands also, what He (God) has joined together let no man put asunder. So you see why I say.

> *"Marriages are made in Heaven,*
> *Marriages is God's doings.*
> *It's Spirituals, it's about Ministry and*
> *God is the perfect match maker."*

DEDICATION:

To my wife Tommie Jean McTizic – Woods, who has been my encourager and motivator for more than fifty – years.

My daughters Dawn and Sheila

My grandson V'oci Oshea

My granddaughters Mallory, Dorian and Addia Toma

To everyone that supported and had the privilege of reading this book .

My prayer is that the content of this book will cause you to consider the sanctity of Marriage that has been ordained by God.

KNOW THIS:

Marriage is God's Doings

Marriage is Spiritual

Marriage is About Ministry

And God is the Perfect Matchmaker

Marriages Are Made In Heaven

ACKNOWLEDGEMENTS

I want to take this opportunity to say to my niece, Ms. Gwendolyn Sain, retired educator of Dayton, Ohio public schools and English Professor of Central State University, Wilberforce, Ohio. Thank you so much, for taking the time to peruse and edit this writing.

I also wish to acknowledge my older sisters; Mrs. Ocie Woods Williams, who has been and continues to be an inspiration to me by the beautiful poems she writes.

And Mrs. Minnie 'Nent' Woods Sain, who treated me like her son. Until I was five years old, I thought she was my mother, even today she seem to think she is my mother.

-bobby woods-

TABLE OF CONTENT

Dedication	7
Marriages Ae Made In Heaven	13
Perfect Gift From God	17
Family Structure	21
Two Made One Flesh	26
Why God Put Adam To Sleep	31
Marriage Is God's Doing / Divorce Is Satan's Doing	35
Marriages Are Made In Heaven God's Doing	36
Divorce an Epidemic Satan's Doing	38
Teaching and Statistics	46
Time For Weeping	51
Serious Statistics	55
What Are We Teaching	61
Unity of Husband and Wife	67
Counseling	75
Counseling Before Marriage	76
Who Is Qualified To Perform Pre - Marital Counseling	76

Purpose For Pre - Marital Counseling	79
Sex Education	83
Sex Before Marriage	84
Dangers of Fornication	85
It's About Sex	87
They Call It Sex	90
Sex In Three Dimensions	95
Why Marriages Fail	101
Becoming Too Common	102
Lying	104
Comparison That's A No - No	106
Baggage From A Previous Marriage	108
Un Forgiveness	110
Over Protective	111
Marriages With Step Children / A Blended Family	112
Secrets and Surprises	115
The God Ordained Marriage	117
Marriage Is For Grown - Ups and It's Forever	118
Same Sex Marriage	120
Definition For The Word Marriage	122

Our God Can Break Generational Curses	**125**
Remember	**126**
Be Alert	**127**
Don't Let Satan Win Again	**128**
Notes	**130**
Contact Information	**134**
Biography (About The Author)	**135**

Thank You for Your Support

-Bobby Woods-

Bobby L. Woods

MARRIAGES ARE MADE IN HEAVEN

Marriages Are Made In Heaven

There is a cliché that I have heard since I was a young child; sometimes sarcastically and in question form "Are marriages made in heaven?" The answer was; an absolute 'NO' or 'NO WAY' Marriages are not made in heaven is what the question/cliché suggests.

I have always accepted this thought as true; I based this on the fact that all marriages, without exceptions, have problems in respect to the husband and wife's relationship. God made husbands and wives one flesh; yet two bodies, two minds, two personalities, two souls and two spirits.

Men and women are similar in many ways, yet different in many ways. Because of these differences all marriages demand work. No marriage will work, for saints or sinners, without being worked on. In other words, unless the married couple is willing to unselfishly compromise their differences, give and give some more, forgive and forgive again and again, the marriage won't work. It just won't work for anybody. Knowing these things made it easy for me to believe the old saying, (the old proverb) "No marriages are not made in heaven".

As I look at the marriage situation today, I see people so in love they can't stand to be without each other, even for a short time. Some say we want to grow old together. Some say, I don't think I would want to live without you. Less than two years later that same couple is saying I don't love you. I want you out of my life. I want a divorce. That's another reason why I believed the old saying, No marriage is made in heaven. Now as I give thought, study, and prayer to the concept of marriage; taking a biblical view, I believe differently. I am totally convinced that godly Marriages are Made In Heaven.

We sometime accuse one another of being match makers. Because many of us (out of concern and compassion) try to choose mates for our children, our friends and people that we care about.

God is literally a match maker.

God actually makes matches for people.

God customizes people for people,

[Just as He did for Adam]

and he does it in heaven.

marriages are made in heaven!

Marriage is Spiritual

Marriage is about Ministry

marriage is God's doing

and let us not forget

marriage is for KEEPS

Marriages Are Made In Heaven

I believe these are some important TRUTHS that are being left out of our teachings on the subjects of marriage and divorce. Some of these truths I have never heard discussed at any church service or bible class. I will try to reveal more of these truths as we go along.

My generation is not teaching these truths. The younger generation doesn't have them. They have never heard these truths. They don't realize that marriage is sacred. They don't know that God brought them together because He has a part and a place for them as a couple in his ministry. They don't know that in marriage they will have to fight together just to keep it together. All they know is that they love each other, and want to be together for the rest of their lives. Because they don't have these truths concerning marriage, their marriages are failing. They are lost and we are not blameless.

Perfect Gift From God

We must understand that the husband and the wife are gifts to one another from God. All good and perfect gifts come from God. He only gives good and perfect gifts.

When God gives you a spouse he is concerned about your work in the ministry. If he gives you anything less than perfection to work with, you could blame him when it didn't work out. James 1:17 says, "Every good gift and every perfect gift is from above, and cometh down from the father of light..." Nobody can point a finger of blame at God.

Adam tried to shift the blame for his disobedience. God had blessed Adam with everything he needed. He had prepared a special place for him eastward in Eden. He was blessed with a beautiful place called the Garden of Eden. God gave him an assignment (ministry) and outlined what He wanted him to do. Genesis 2:15 And the Lord God took the man, and put him into the Garden of Eden to dress it and to keep it. God would come down just to pay Adam a visit from time to time.

Letting my imagination run free, I can see God In my mind visiting Adam walking and talking, I can hear God telling Adam about Gabriel, Raphael, Michael, and other angels. I can hear Him in my imagination, of course, telling Adam what's going on, and how things are in Heaven.

Speaking words of encouragement to Adam telling him how much he loved him and his wife. Telling Adam how much he appreciates him taking care things on earth. I can imagine God Saying things such as; you are doing a good job. Keep doing what you are doing. Don't allow yourself to be distracted. God and man fellowshipping in the garden in the cool of the day, what a beautiful picture. Fellowship is a beautiful thing to have with anyone you care about. But to have fellowship with God is awesome.

One day God came to visit Adam in the garden. This time He did not find him doing ministry, (working his assignment). God found Adam and Eve hiding among the trees. They were trying to hide their nakedness with fig leaves; because they had sinned and were ashamed to stand before God.

As they were being evicted from the garden, Adam tried to put the blame on his wife and God. Genesis 3:12 He (Adam) said, "That woman whom thou gavest to be with me, she gave me of the tree..." God didn't bother to respond to Adam's accusation. He just kicked them out of the garden.

God placed an angel with a flaming sword to guard the gate so Adam and Eve could not return. If they had continued eating from the tree of life they would not die. If you relate this story to us at this time, Jesus is our tree that gives us eternal life.

Early on I said, God only gives good and perfect gifts. Don't misunderstand me. I did not say God would give you a perfect man or woman. No one's perfect in the flesh. God considers not the flesh but the spirit. We all have our flaws and faults. That's why we must be willing to give and forgive.

God knows exactly what we need in a spouse to do the job that he has assigned us. We will never be perfect people in this life, but we can be perfect mates, if we let God do the match making. Notwithstanding God only looks on the heart. If you have a pure heart, a heart to please God, you are perfect in his site.

God knows your purpose in ministry, and He knows exactly what type of person to put in your life to bring you to that place. A friend of mine's got married having no doubt that the woman he chose was God's choice for him. It wasn't very long before the woman put God out of her life and caused much pain and chaos in the relationship. The brother was dismayed thinking that there had to have been a mistake in choosing. I know God doesn't make mistakes. He had not made a mistake in this choice either. What the brother failed to understand was that his ministry would be helping people who were hurting. This was something that he had to go through. God was making and molding him, getting him ready for his ministry. The gift was perfect for the purpose. Sometimes God allows the minister to feel the same pain as those that he/she is to minister to, so that he might have patience and longsuffering for those who he/she will minister to. God works in mysterious ways. We will never be able to totally understand His ways. Isaiah 55:8 For My thoughts are not your thoughts, neither are your ways my ways, says the Lord. For as the heavens are higher than the earth. So are my ways higher than your ways, and my thoughts than your thoughts.

The human mind can never totally understand the fullness of who God is. Hosea 6:3 But He will give you insight if you follow on to know Him. You can have fellowship with him. If your ways please him he will give you the desires of your heart. Yes, He will give you the spouse that you need to fulfill your purpose and mission.

Bobby L. Woods

Family Structure

Structure is a word you might hear over and over all day on any construction site. Structure is one of the most important factors in the construction of any building. Be it a small house, or a great skyscraper. The way it's put together (structured) determines the strength, and the endurance of the building. You might have the best building materials, but if your building is not properly structured, it won't endure the pressure that it should.

Please believe me. God is totally concerned about family structure. When Adam and Eve had to be removed from the Garden of Eden for their disobedience, God cursed the earth that living and survival would not be so easy. It would cost sweat (work). Because God loved them, He gave them something that would make living and survival possible. God gave them family structure.

He made Adam the head and commanded Eve to submit to Adam's rule. This was not a punishment for Eve neither was he showing favor to Adam. God was organizing the family and giving it structure, a sound base, a foundation for successful living. Family Does Matter. Everything we are and everything we will ever become or accomplish as a people has its roots coming out of the family structure. Family structure is the basis for family survival and marriage is the basis for family structure. In order for any organization to be successful, it has to have structure. Everyone needs to know their place and their position. Everyone needs to know who the leader is or who is in charge. This is what I call STRUCTURE.

If there is no structure you can expect chaos and confusion. The Bible tells us that God is not the author of confusion but of peace. I am so sorry that so many brothers have a misunderstanding as to what God wanted when he said the man would be ruler of the wife. Some think God is saying the man is the boss; he is to dominate his wife. In other words, the woman is inferior to the man. God did not make any person superior or inferior to another. He was delegating responsibilities and setting guidelines or order, for the sake of peace. If God wanted the woman to be inferior to the man, I think he would have taken power and authority from her, but He did not.

> *God commanded woman with her authority*
> *to submit to her husband, this way everybody knows*
> *their place so there will be no power struggle.*

We must understand also that along with authority come responsibility. God is delegating responsibility: The man is to lead, to protect, and to provide for his wife and family. May I say to you my sister; if your husband respects God's Word he will respect you. You have the best position in the family origin, so don't fight family structure be proud of it.

We are crying, complaining, and praying about the condition of our economy. That's not a bad thing. We should be concerned about our economy. I want you to know that the condition of our family structure is worse than the condition of our economy; and Family Structure is much more important.

God did not give them (Adam and Eve) money when he sent them away. He gave them something more precious than money could ever be. He gave them Family Structure. The family structure that God gives us is more important than our economy, or anything else we might possess. Nothing is impossible for the family that stays grounded in its God given structure because they will stay together and God will be with them.

After the water had gone down following the flood, in the days of Noah, God had planned for the families of Noah to separate and spread to all parts the earth. Instead of following God's plan they had plans of their own. They decided to stay together and make a name for themselves by building a city and a tower that would reach into heaven. God himself said, if I don't stop them they will succeed because they are together (have structure). God confused their language. They could not continue building because they could not communicate. Part of this tower stands today and is called, 'The Towel of Babel'.

An old proverb says, "Together we stand, divided we will fall." When the Family Structure fails, the family itself fails. When families fail, communities fail. When communities fail, cities, states and countries fail. When countries fail their money becomes confetti. Yes that's how important family is.

Living together as husband and wife without the marriage commitment is not the answer. It has proven to be unprofitable in every way and to everyone that's involved. It is not God's way. It's fornication. It is sin.

Fornication is sin, and it is destructive. Divorce is like cancer eating into God's plan for the family structure causing it to weaken. Divorce is one of the strongest weapons Satan has to use against families. It has a destructive effect on communities and countries. Divorces don't just dissolve marriage relations, it destroys families. It is a great loss for the family and for the community. Families separating have a negative effect on the world that we live in.

God's will and plan for the family is; father, mother and children living together as a unit, loving supporting, and respecting one another. The parents are to teach/train the children that they might know how to be parent to their children and to survive as a unit. God gave parents a commandment; Proverb 22:6 "Train up your children in the way they should go and when they are old they will not depart from it."

Bishop G. E. Paterson tells us what the word train means in that scripture. He says it means; to run the same drill over and over until doing the right thing becomes a habit.

As parents we cannot teach one thing while doing the opposite. In order to be effective, we must teach by precept and example. What we do and the way we live before our children speaks louder than what we say to our children.

Two Made One Flesh

The Bible declares that in marriage the husband and his wife become one flesh, Genesis 2:24. This is a mystery, so says the Bible. I have no explanation as to how two people can become one flesh except the fact that God said it. God is not a man that he should lie. If God said it, that settles it. No other explanation is necessary.

The question that has always been in the back of my mind is why did he say one flesh? Why not one spirit? A husband and his wife can be miles apart yet one flesh because God says so. We know that marriage is spiritual, so why did he not say the man and his wife would be one soul in marriage? I have not found the answer to this question in the Bible, but I will give my thoughts on the matter. Even though marriage is spiritual, it pertains to the fleshly part of man, the part that is not eternal. Man is three parts:

The flesh is the part that came from the earth. It is earthy and will go back to the earth at death and be dissolved. So will marriage be dissolved at death. There is no sex or marriage after this life. Death dissolves marriage vows, legal responsibilities and benefits. Marriage is for here and now in the earth. I do believe as Christians we will see our spouses in heaven, and we will know them but not as husband and wife. We will be spiritual beings, not needing any of the things that we need now while in the earth, including marriage.

Matthew 22:24-30, A Sadducee came to Jesus with a question concerning a woman who had been married seven times to seven brothers, not at one time of course. The point is they had all died and the women died also. The Sadducee wanted to know of the seven brothers whose wife would she be in the resurrection? Jesus answers the question in verse 30, "…in the resurrection they neither marry, nor are given in marriage."

Back to the question; why did God not say they would become one soul? This is my answer. If God had said the man and his wife would become one soul that would be an eternal union because the soul will never see death. And these two souls would be together throughout eternity, which means if one goes to heaven or hell, because they are made one, they both would end up in the same place Ezekiel 18:4 "Behold all souls are mine; as the soul of the father, so also the soul of the son is mine: the soul that sinneth it shall die." In marriage, God unites the flesh, not the soul. One person cannot be responsible for another person's soul.

Married couples are bound to each other in the flesh with a spiritual/divine binding. Marriage vows constitute both a legal and a spiritual binding. These vows are endorsed by the laws of God and the laws of man. These vows are what I like to call contracts. They make each party responsible for each other, through hard times, good times, and bad times until death. However, should one break the contract, by being unfaithful, disloyal or disrespectful to their vows, man's law gives the violated spouse a way out. It's called DIVORCE; this is where man's laws and God's laws separate. God's word says who GOD HAS JOINED TOGETHER let no man put asunder. This means, when God brings two people together in marriage, there should be no need for a way out/divorce. When God brings two people together it will be a perfect match; two imperfect people, yet a perfect match, to meet the purpose. The (God given) vows that people make in marriage are more than contracts. They are covenants. Covenants are much stronger than contracts. A contract, is an agreement between two people. If one party defaults it automatically lets the other person out of their contract or promise. The marriage covenant is a solemn promise, made by both parties before God. The covenant stands alone. It has no strings attached, and demands nothing of the other party but to accept it. People are writing their own vows and saying them to one another, during the ceremony. Often disregarding the biblical principles ordained by God.

This is the marital vows for Christians:

I,_____ take thee____, to be my wedded wife/husband, to have and to hold from this day forward, for better or worse, for richer or poorer, in sickness, and health, to love and cherish till death us do we part, according to God's Holy ordinance; and there to I pledge thee my faith.

The above statement is a covenant, not just a contract. Each individual makes a covenant promise to the other and to God!

MARRAGES ARE SPIRITUAL
MARRIAGES ARE ABOUT MINISTRY
MARRIAGES ARE MADE IN HEAVEN

Marriage is so much more than most people perceive it to be. It is more than two people making vows to one another; its more than two people becoming one flesh. Marriage is more than two people seeking to please each other. I don't think anyone can explain the full truth of what marriage is. It's a mystery, it's sacred, and it's miraculous.

Marriage is God's doing and it has purpose. Looking at the big picture, I find that we all have a part to play in God's overall plan. He knows exactly what each person need to successfully perform the job assignment. God orchestrated marriage and ordained marriage before the foundation of the world. God's big plan is to minister to the world, bringing provision and salvation to all men, redeeming man back to himself.

When God saves a person and puts his spirit in them, he is getting them ready to be a part in his ministry. One should count themselves blessed and highly favored when God gives them a spouse, but know that it is not all about them. It is part of his plan of salvation for the world.

Many people go through life not realizing who they are, or how they fit into God's plan. Some get saved, get married, find a church home and attend faithfully, on their way to heaven not knowing that their experiences are not about themselves, but they are part of God's master plan. It's like the low level drug dealers who deals drugs on the street in his neighborhood. He is thinking he's independent, not realizing he is part of organized crime worldwide.

There are no independent Christians. If you are saved today, you are part of God's team called to spread the gospel of Jesus Christ to the world. If he has given you a spouse, it is to aid you and partner with you in the ministry. The husband and his wife are made one for a purpose. They are to be helpers together!

Bobby L. Woods

Why God Put Adam to Sleep

When God was ready to make Adam a wife, he caused a deep sleep to come upon him (put the flesh to sleep). It was not because Adam needed to take a nap or rest. I don't think God put Adam to sleep because the operation would be so painful. If God could open him up go inside of him take out a rib, close him up and not leave a scar, I think he could have done it without pain. Don't you?

The Bible doesn't say why God put Adam to sleep. I would like to share my thought on the matter. I believe God put Adam to sleep so the flesh (Adam's Flesh) could not interfere. I do believe, if Adam had had anything to do with what his wife would be like or look like, he would have messed it up big time. Like we do today when we take the responsibility upon ourselves to find and choose our spouse. God knew what was best for Adam. And God knows what's best for you and me. The best thing we can do for ourselves is to agree with him. Adam said, "This is now bone of my bones, and flesh of my flesh: and she shall be called Woman." God said the two of them would be one flesh.

Because of the translation of our Bible into the English language and the way it is written, one could easily come away thinking God put his hands inside of Adam's body took out a rib and made a woman. As a result, they are one flesh. God didn't make anything with his hands. Everything He made He simply spoke it into existence. St. John 1:3 declares, it was the Word that made everything that was made. Jesus was that Word. Adam and Eve were one flesh because God spoke it. We today become one flesh in marriage because God said it. Please, please, don't take marriage lightly. God doesn't.

In case there are questions, our marriages today in the sight of God are just as sacred and profound as the marriage between Adam and Eve.

> *Marriage is serious business,*
> *Marriage is spiritual business,*
> *Marriage is God's business,*
> *Marriage is beautiful.*
> *Marriages are made in Heaven*

The church community is not taking marriage seriously. We are forgetting the spiritual side of marriage. We are turning it into something that's not so beautiful. Jesus said to his disciples, "Occupy till I come", Meaning take charge until I come back.

Jesus says that we are the light of the world. This means, we are to be an example to the world. We should show them the way. We should show them how marriage should be done. Christians should show the world what God had in mind when he instituted marriage. People should be inspired by seeing the relationships of Christian married couples causing them to say I want that. Instead of wanting what we have, they are saying no, no, no! I don't think I want that. I don't think I can handle that.

Marriage is too much stress.

Marriage is too much pain.

Marriage is too much trouble.

Marriage doesn't work.

This is the message we are sending our youth. God is becoming weary of our wicked ways. We need to crucify the flesh. (Paul said I die daily). We need to put the flesh to sleep and let God give us the spouse that fits the ministry.

Marriages Are Made In Heaven

MARRIAGE IS GOD'S DOING

DIVORCE IS SATAN'S DOING

Marriages Are Made In Heaven
God's Doing's

I believe marriages are made in heaven, and it is God's doing because man has very little to do with it. That applies to the bride and the groom as well. We go to the judge or preacher and repeat marital vows. We perform the marital ceremony which constitutes a legal binding, but marriage is God's doing, it's divine. If a person is called by God to be married (some are not), God chooses the spouse, and God chooses the time. We don't get to choose any of these things. It's all God's doing. One may choose a spouse, but they will need God's approval. Marriage is holy; that's God's doing. Marriage is sacred; that's God's doing. Marriage is making two people one flesh. I know that's God's doing! Yes, I believe marriage is made in heaven and is Gods doing because it was God that orchestrated marriage, It was not man's idea. Adam didn't ask for a wife; he never thought of that. This was God's doing, and it was not done just for the couple to enjoy each other in a sexual relationship, but for the ministry. Of course sex between the husband and his wife was God's way of populating the earth. Bearing children, rearing children, and training children to love, fear and obey God was already in the plan for Adam and Eve and for us.

Ministry always starts at home. I believe marriage is made in heaven because the Bible says in Proverbs 19:14 "A prudent wife is from the Lord." You might inherit houses and riches from your earthly father, but if you have a prudent wife she is a gift that comes from God. The judge or the preacher can pronounce a couple man and wife, but it is God that joins the two together and causes them to become one flesh. And He says let no man separate you.

One of the biggest mistakes married people make is, they draw invisible lines and dare their spouses to cross them. Some do it shortly after the wedding. Some do it before, but sooner or later most young couples will get around to making that mistake. They lay out a list of things that they will not tolerate; they say to their spouse, if you ever do this or that, it will be the end. You are out of here, or I'm out of here, this marriage will be over. They make up their own list of rules. What they don't understand is marriage is God's doing, and our rules don't apply. How soon we forget the marriage vow that says, "till death do we part." If we want our marriage to work, we must use God's rules for guidelines. Also, when a person voices the things he or she won't take, they give Satan a target to zoom in on concerning their marriage. Satan is not omnipotent. He doesn't know everything, as God does, but he can hear the words that come out of your mouth. And Satan doesn't forget what he hears. The Bible says, make no room for Satan. These kinds of statements give Satan just enough room to get his foot in the door, and he will work with that. Take the mindset that marriage is forever and be determined to make it work.

When God brings two people together, Satan gets busy running to and fro, trying to figure out what it will take to break or destroy this union. When he hears one spouse tell the other what he/she won't take Satan knows exactly what he needs to do, and he does not procrastinate. As soon as he get, or should I say, as soon as you give him that information he goes to work on your case. I don't claim to have all the answers, or understand all the facts and mysteries about marriage, but I do know, it is more spiritual than natural.

I do know it was designed by God; I do know that one of its greatest purposes is to enhance one another in the work of the ministry. I also know that the divorce problem is having a negative effect on the entire world. Yes it's a global problem, and it's getting worse every day. That's a truth that cannot be denied. People are changing marital partners as one would change an automobile or a household appliance. Others are afraid to get married. Children are being molested, used, abused, and even killed every day because they do not have the protection of both parents in the home. Children are the real victims when there is a separation or a divorce.

Divorce an Epidemic

Satan's Doings

Divorce is at an epidemic proportion in the secular community and in the church community as well. Statistics say more than 50% of all marriages in the secular community will end in divorce within a few years. When I heard that report I was taken off of my feet. That was an alarming report. I didn't want to believe it was true. I kept hoping to hear that the report was false or a mistake, but that didn't happen. Instead, I was informed that there is a greater percentage of divorce cases in the church community than there are in the secular community. This is absolutely, positively tragic. But, statics have proven that there are less divorce cases among non-Christians than there are of Christians; those who are professing to be disciples of Jesus Christ and are called by his name.

> *What? That's crazy!*
> *How can this be true?*
> *Where did we get off track?*
> *Something is terribly wrong.*
> *This is heart breaking!*
> *It's praying time!*
> *Yes! it is praying time.*

Can we be disciples of Jesus if we can't love and forgive one another? How can we say that we love God whom we have not seen, at any time and hate (can't forgive) our brother (spouses) that we see daily? If we don't forgive our brother or sister who transgresses against us, God will not forgive our transgressions against him. That's a biblical truth. We teach that truth; we live by this truth; except when we have problems in our marriage. When there is a problem with our marriage, we don't try to forgive one another. We get divorced and try to forget one another.

As Christians we are called out to be an example to the world. II Peter 2:9 "But you are a chosen generation, a royal priesthood, an holy nation, a peculiar people; that you should show forth the praises of him who hath called you out of darkness into his marvelous light:" If we, the people of God, are doing worse than the world, something has gone very wrong.

Where is the light? Where is the salt?

Where is the example? Where is the praise?

Where is the love?

Where is the hope for those who walk in darkness?

What happened to the light that the bible speaks of in Matthew 5:14 "Ye are the light of the world. A city that is set on an hill cannot be hid."

The divorce situation is extremely serious, and the church is not saying enough about it. We hear more talk about the divorce problems in the secular news than we do in the church. This is so sad that I can hardly keep a dry eye as I write. The church should set the example; instead the church is following the examples of Hollywood. If there is a problem with the first marriage, we just walk away find another partner, and get married again. If the second one doesn't work, we repeat the cycle. Where is God in all of this? Where is He? This is happening in our churches not only among laymen but by those who are in leadership as well. Not regarding the clause in the marriage vow, that says, "Till death do we part."

Question: If two Christians are married and one backslides, does that give the other one the right to get a divorce and marry someone else? The answer to that question is NO.

The word backslide carries a meaning of defeat. It simply means that Satan has defeated that spouse and pulled them back into a state of sin. They are bound by the power of darkness. At this point, they need you (the stronger spouse) more than ever before. They need you to be fasting and praying and fighting for their freedom. That's not an option for the stronger spouse. It's an obligation. It's a command. That's what marriage is about. Romans 15:1-2, we then that are strong ought to bear the infirmities of the weak, and not be pleasers of ourselves. Of course, it won't be easy to fight for someone who is possibly fighting against you. This test will be super hard if there is a third party involved, or romance involving a third party. I already know that most people won't be able to receive that last statement. Most people don't understand what the word marriage means.

That is called sacrifice.

That is what marriage is.

That is called long suffering.

That is called commitment.

That is what makes Christians different.

That is what makes us a peculiar people.

That is honoring the fact that you are one flesh.

These are some things we should consider before we say, "I do". You don't walk away from a love-one. Neither do you allow them to push you away when Satan has his foot on their neck. The first thing you should remember is; this is a soul that you are fighting for; second, this is your sister or brother; third, this is your spouse and they should be closer to you than anyone on earth.

God has made you one flesh. You simply have to keep fighting for them. Even if they leave, you should continue fasting, praying, and fighting, giving them time to find themselves, time to find their way back to God and to you. They can't come back to you if you are married to someone else.

You keep fasting. You keep holding on.

You suffer long. You keep praying.

You keep fighting until God says enough.

It is my plan never to backslide again. Yes, I did say again. I can't say that I have not backslidden since the Lord saved me. Thank God for his grace and mercy. I would hate to think my spouse would walk away and leave me defeated and at the mercy of Satan. Apostle Paul says, "And unto the married I command, yet not I, but the Lord, "Let not the wife depart from her husband: But and if she depart, let her remain unmarried, or be reconciled to her husband: and let not the husband put away his wife." 2 Corinthians 7:10-11.

How can any Christian get around scripture such as these and not feel condemned? Do we understand what marriage is? Let me tell you what it is not:

Marriage is not a trial and error situation.

It is not something you can jump into hoping that this is the right thing to do, hoping this is the right person to do it with and the right time.

If it's not the right one or the right time you can't use divorce as an eraser to wipe it all away. You can't delete it and try something else. You have to know going in that it is the right person and the right time. The only way you can be sure of these things is by seeking God before going in.

Marriage is ministry. Like any ministry one need to be sure before starting. Proverb 3:5-6 tells us how to do that. "Lean not to your own understanding, but in all thy ways acknowledge him, (God) and he shall direct thy paths." It's not terribly surprising to see non-Christians take the attitude of trial and error, concerning marriage. If one doesn't work try another. Because their reason for getting marriage is to fulfill their own needs, lusts and desires. These are all selfish reasons. Saints know that marriage is more than fulfilling personal needs or desires.

Marriage is a God thing. One can plainly see that the church community is failing God in this area. We are simply forgetting that we should glorify God in our marriages. The Bible gives us direction. David said God will be a lamp unto my feet and a light unto my path. It is heart breaking to see how far we have gone in the wrong direction with regard to marriage.

We have strayed from the path.

We have strayed from God's word,

We have strayed from bible instructions

We have strayed from God's righteousness

We have established our own righteousness

and standards as it relates to marriage and divorce.

God Will JUDGE!

Yes, God will forgive, but He is a righteous judge.

As it relates to marriage and the commitment thereof, we the people of God are losing ground. We are too thin skinned, we are much too proud, we are self-centered, and we are concerned with what others will say. We are not concerned with what God is saying. We are following the way of the sinner. I'm saddened and concerned because many leaders are falling into this snare of, pleasing themselves. God commissioned the preachers to show his people their sins and their transgressions. But you can't help someone else to get free when you are bound yourself.

There is a pastor in my hometown that was thought of as a great man of God, a great leader in the community. He had a beautiful fast growing church. This man I'm told had been married for several years. He fell in love or lust with another woman in his congregation and divorced his wife. He married the other woman and continued preaching as if nothing was wrong. This man continued as pastor at the same church where the x-wife was still a member.

Teaching and Statistics

Let's take a second look at our teaching concerning the subjects of marriage and divorce. We must examine what we are teaching. We must compare it to the Bible to be assured that we are teaching scripture, and not tradition nor denominational doctrines. Not what fit our situation and not what we think about it. We must teach what God says about it. God's word is true, it doesn't matter what we think. As we teach the Word of God we must be direct and straight forward. We must not vary to the right or left. Let God be true but every man a liar. As it is written Roman 3:4b. We are not without teachings on the subject of marriage. The churches are teaching on marriage in Bible classes and special seminars. Parents are teaching in the homes and grandparents are teaching the children. Everybody is teaching and giving advice on the subject of marriage. Yet the divorce rate is at an all-time high and rising. It's so high in these United States that the government is getting concerned. Law-makers are seeking ways of keeping families together. County health departments are sponsoring or holding anger management classes and marriage counseling classes trying to keep families together.

If we have more than 50% of marriages ending in divorce, my guess is that we have 25% or more dysfunctional marriages. These are couples who choose to remain in the relationship for the sake of the children; for security; for legal or political reasons. Yet they are not satisfied. They are living together in the same house but are not together in a relationship. They are not one by any aspect of the word. These couples really want out of the marriage. This leaves less than 25% happy, healthy and prosperous marriages. What a sad, SAD picture, especially among those who are called Christians. Can you believe that!

We have 50% failed marriages. That's exactly 50% more than it should be. Marriage is God's doing. What God does should never fail. (Let no man put asunder).

Concerning dysfunctional marriages, I said my guess is that we have 25% or more. Among this group are those who fuss and fight at home. When in public, they put on this little charade, acting and making believe all is well. It's impossible to put a number on this group. It could possibly be much more than 25%. So we use an educated guess. We really don't need an exact number to know that we are in real trouble. With more than 50% of marriages ending in divorce, 25% or more dysfunctional, that is a 75% or maybe 80 % or more negative rate. Any company, organization or business having a 75% negative rating is out of business and considered to be a failure. The marriage institution is a failure. It's not working. It is broken. It needs fixing. And IT NEEDS FIXING NOW. I know that there is nothing wrong with the institution of marriage itself.

Marriage is good. Marriage is God's doing but there is something terribly wrong with our concept of marriage. There is something missing in the teaching. We do not understand what God had planned for us concerning marriage. One of the problems is we are turning a deaf ear to God's Word; the Holy Ghost is grieved; God is vexed; and I'm afraid we are getting ourselves in big trouble.

We have set a poor example for our youth. They are afraid to get married. Seeing the divorce rate escalate and the pain and agony that follows, they are convinced that marriage doesn't work. They are choosing to live together without the commitment of marriage. We call it shacking. Statics has it that four out of every ten young women who get married have already co-habited with a man. That's not God's way. It's certainly not God's will for our youth. It's degrading, It's by-passing the anchor of family structure. Our youth won't know better unless we teach them better.

Some states in this country have laws in place that gives a degree of binding to two people who live together for a number of years as husband and wife. It's called Common Law Marriage. The common law marriage requires no commitments, no ceremony and no wedding. It requires no promises and no vows.

The man and woman just live together as husband and wife for a number of years and the law automatically takes place. Is this marriage pleasing to God? I think not! Any so called marriage taking place without vows of total commitment is no marriage in Gods sight. This marriage is not God centered.

It's not God's doing.

It's not good for ministry.

It's not one that's made in Heaven.

It has no godly foundation.

This kind of marriage will never have God's approval or blessing on it. If I may advise you don't go down that road. It's a dead in street. If you want to be married do it right. Do it God's way.

I agree with what many are saying. It seems like people get along better just living together without commitment than they do when they are married. I've heard men and women as well say, once you say "I do" that spouse thinks they own you. Well, no one person can own another in this country, but there is and should be a deep sense of belonging.

There is a song that says" I give myself to you." That's what marriage is. The man and his wife belong to one another. 1 Corinthians 7:4, the wife hath not power of her own body, but the husband: and likewise also the husband hath not power of his own body, but the wife. It's a good thing, and I say again, it's a good thing. It's not a matter of owning or possessing one another but freely and continually giving oneself to the other. In marriage you are more than two people belonging to one another. The Bible says you are not two anymore but one flesh.

Marriages Are Made In Heaven

God makes you one. That's what we should be teaching.

Question! Is marriage good? Yes, by all means, but you need to know what the word marriage means. It means you have come into a covenant relationship with God concerning this person. It means you have promised to love this person for the rest of your life. It means you have promised to be there for this person through good and hard times for as long as you live. It doesn't matter how much you want to be married or how much you think you need to be married. If you are not ready to make a lifetime commitment, marriage is not good for you. It won't work. This is what we should practice and this is what we should teach!

Bobby L. Woods

Time for Weeping

God's people have chosen to believe that divorce is the answer to our marital problems. I have thought about it, and I've prayed about it. I have come to the conclusion that divorce is not the answer. Divorce is a problem. It is like a fungus or an incurable disease. It has woven itself deeply into the fabric of our society. The only foreseeable hope for change is for those who have a relationship with God to go on their face before Him. We need to cry out in intercessory prayer for the people of God concerning this issue. The prayers of the righteous really do avail much.

If the Prophet Jeremiah who was called the weeping prophet was here today, I do believe he would take up a wailing as never before. When he could shed no more tears for the people of God, he would call for the mourning women that they may come, and the conning women that they may come, and make haste and take up a wailing for us; as it is written in Jeremiah 9:17-18.

This is so sad that it brings tears to my eyes as I write. How did we, while walking so close to God get so far from what God had planned for us concerning our marriage relationships? How did we come to the conclusion that divorce is the answer? If divorce is the answer why does it hurt so badly? Why does the pain last so long? Why do most

Christian divorcees regret it later? Why does it reach out so far and hurt so many others outside of the marriage? Why does it destroy so many of our children? Why is the church so quiet concerning this? Is the church community asleep? Can we recognize the work of the enemy? Can we or must we accept defeat? Is it time to fight back? Is it time to take back what the Devil has stolen? I say it's time for a revolution, don't you? If your answer is yes, then where do we start?

Before we get started on this journey, let's go first into our secret closet and pray. This problem will only be solved by much fasting and praying. So, let's strengthen ourselves in the Lord with prayer and fasting. It's time to come before the altar of God weeping and crying out to God that He will give us understanding, direction, strength and courage to fight this battle. God is our only hope.

The children of Israel were slaves in Egypt for more than four hundred years. It seemed there was no hope of ever being free again. They had no hope of ever being in their home land again. The Bible says in Exodus 2:23b ...they cried, and their cry came up unto God. vs. 24a and God heard their groaning, and God remembered his covenant with Abraham, with Isaac, with Jacob... and so on as the story goes.

The people cried out to God, and He sent Moses to deliver them. He brought them out of the land of Egypt, across the Red Sea, though the wilderness. He allowed them to see a land flowing with milk and honey, where they would have houses and cities that they did not build, and fields ready for harvest.

God is no respecter of person. What He did for Israel He will do for us. Hebrews 13:8 says, "Jesus Christ the same yesterday and today, and forever." If the people of God will cry out to Him;

> *He will send help.*
>
> *He will deliver.*
>
> *He will forgive our sins.*
>
> *He will save our land.*
>
> *He will save our marriages.*

2 Chronicles 7:14 says, "If my people, which are called by my name, shall humble themselves, and pray, and seek my face, and turn from their wicked ways; then will I hear from heaven, and will forgive their sins, and will heal their land." Vs.15 Now mine eyes shall be open, and mine ears attent unto the prayer that is made in this place.

> *Yes, it's crying time again.*
>
> *It's time for intercession.*
>
> *It's time to be awakened.*

It's time to realize that marriage is made in heaven.

It's time to realize that marriage is about ministry.

It's time to realize that marriage is spiritual.

It's time to realize that marriage is sacred.

It's time to realize that marriage is God's doing.

It's time to realize that marriage is for keeps.

Serious Statistics

Satan doesn't play fair; he doesn't wait for our children to grow up or to mature. He starts trying to destroy them as soon as they are born. He sometimes goes after our children before they are born. If we don't protect our children, they don't have much of a chance for success or survival in this dark sin stricken society.

When a father doesn't pay child support, we call him a dead beat dad. A deadbeat is one who will selfishly put his desires before his child's needs. Fathers should be role models.

Listen to these facts and numbers. Suicide among teens is at an all-time high.

Statics has it:

66% of all teen suicide victims are products of single parent homes, or homes without a father.

90% of all teenage runaways come out of homes where there are no fathers.

85% of all children that exhibit behavioral disorders are the product of fatherless homes.

71% of all children in state institutions are from fatherless homes.

85% of all youths in prison are fatherless home victims.

These numbers are frightening, downright, bone chilling scary. Did I make my point?

The father figure is absolutely essential in the home, and in the lives of his children. The word of God says, if a man won't take care of his family, he has departed from the faith. It goes on to say, that he is worse than an infidel. My interpretation is; 'He is a fool and he is evil.'

Some of our men are ignorant enough to think that when they pay child support, they have done enough. Some try to avoid paying that. They say that's too much to ask of them. Some of the real deadbeats will refuse a public job in order to avoid paying child support.

There are others who really try not to be deadbeat dads. They pay their child support, give the child money, buy them clothing and other things. They occasionally take them places and spend time with them on weekends. Now they feel really good about themselves, saying within themselves; I do more for my child than the average divorced fathers. I do my best and that's enough. Is that really enough?

Well, I think not. What this father is doing is all good. And these are some things any divorced father should do. It might be the best many can do, but is it enough? I am afraid it isn't. All a person can do, is all they can do. I think it is impossible to do enough for your child when the father is living in one place and the child lives in another.

If you ask what is enough, the most important thing a father can do is BE THERE for his children. He was there for the making of the baby, he should be there during labor pains, and delivery, midnight feedings, and for diaper changes, Be there to hear the child's first words, to see them take their first step. Be there to read bedtime stories, Be there to hear their prayers at bedtime, Be there to chase the ghosts out of the bedroom after a nightmare, Be there for the child's first ballgame, and school plays. Be there if you have nothing to give, just be there, JUST BE THERE!!

Brothers before you think about making a baby, think about making provisions to BE THERE. In other words make sure you are in a sound marriage before bringing a child into the world. God's plan for the family is; father, mother, and the children to be one unit. Every child needs a FATHER first and other male/father figure in their life. They need grandfather, uncle, older brother, pastor, teacher, even, the old man across the street. Every child needs a man in their life. Judging by what I have seen during my lifetime, girls need the father figure more than boys. If there is no father figure she won't know how to judge men when she becomes an adult.

I sincerely applaud those women who are doing their best to raise their children without a father in the home. It is a challenge but, with help from God, the children can turn out just fine. But it will take God's help, for with God, all things are possible. Some children are being broken in their spirit. Some are being literally destroyed altogether. This happens for the most part because parents don't understand that the side effects of divorce are very serious and sometime deadly, for the children. This is a harsh saying but, somebody has to say it.

Somebody has to wake us up. Someone has to bring us back into reality. You can close your eyes and imagine life to be easy, that everything is beautiful, lovely and full of peace, but when you wake up and come to yourself the bitter truth will be standing there. God wants the family to be together; Father, mother and children all together as one unit.

truth is; life is not always easy.

you don't just dream the life you want to live.

you have to make the life you want to live.

Marriage isn't easy but it's worth the trouble. These are some issues that premarital counseling should bring to the table because people don't know how serious this is. If they did I'm sure that many would not be as anxious to get married. Others would think twice before seeking a divorce.

By talking to people who have been through the divorce process, I'm finding that most divorces occur because of trivial things and for selfish reasons. There is no room in marriage for selfishness, especially where children are involved. Husbands and wives are being divorced because one hurt the others feelings. One said or did something in the presence of their friends that was embarrassing to the other. One gained weight or lost weight and became not as attractive as before. One got old; one lost his job. One goes back to school and gets a degree, so now they are not on the same level. Some decide, because they are not happy, they just don't want to be married any more. Things change and people change.

These kinds of things are happening in most marriages. Then there are the two big ones: infidelity and finance. I must admit some of these are serious charges, and should not be happening in any marriage. Yet they are all selfish reasons.

When children are involved their welfare must be considered first, even if it means that the parents have to go through some hurt or suffering. That's why it is so very important to know that marriage is God's doing. We must follow his rules and guidelines and allow him to choose our spouse. Even then there will be problems, but the marriage can work.

Statics says more than 50% of all marriages will end in divorce for saints and sinners alike. This is happening because people are not willing to do what has to be done to change this number. It can be changed. I can't speak for the world, but saints must make this change.

I'll offer you this helpful pledge:

I will fast and pray.

I will seek God night and day.

I will listen to what He has to say.

I will do marriage His way.

I will give and forgive.

I'm determined not to become another statistic.

I am determined to make my marriage work

What Are We Teaching?

We are teaching what we believe to be God's Word concerning family, but without positive results.

None whatsoever!

We are not being heard.

We are not being believed.

What can we do now?

Where do we go from here?

Should we keep moving down the same path? Hoping we are headed in the right direction?

Hoping things will get better?

Must we keep doing the same things and hope for different results? I think not, life and time are too precious to play the guessing game.

Any time you are not sure that

you are moving in the right direction

is a good time to stand still

and get some directions from above.

Again, what are we teaching? I think it's time to step back and take a good look at what we are teaching. As I critique the literature that's being circulated, attend the seminars and the classes that are being taught in our churches; I find that our people, for the most part, are receiving sound information and good advice. But the facts remain. The more we preach and teach on marriage relationships, the higher the divorce rates becomes in our communities. That's a fact that cannot be denied.

We are teaching the truth but not getting positive results. My question is, are we teaching the whole truth and nothing but truth? Are we walking in the truth that we are teaching?

Are we teaching truth without any compromise? Our people are not being helped. Let's face the fact that we are not helping them in this area. It seems nobody has the answers to this problem, and nobody knows where to find the answers.

Many of us are hiding our heads in the sand, hoping the problem will go away. Some are throwing in the towel, literally giving up on the marriage/divorce situation. Some are coping out; because we don't have all the answers. We are saying, it has always been this way, and it will always be this way, and there is nothing anybody can do about it. Well, I beg to differ. These are misleading quotes or statements; half-truths, is what I call them. It has not always been this way or this serious, and it doesn't have to remain this way. There is something we can do about it. We know that separation or divorce is not what God had planned for his people from the beginning.

In the book of Matthew Chapter 19:7, the Pharisees came to Jesus tempting him and asked; Is it lawful for a man to put away his wife for every cause? His argument was, Moses commanded them to give their wives a writing of divorcement, and to put her away. Matthews 19:8 Jesus said unto them, "Moses because of the hardness of your hearts (not able to forgive), suffered you to put away your wives: but from the beginning it was not so." With this being true, we know that there must be answers somewhere.

> *Scientists haven't discovered the answer.*
>
> *Law makers don't have the answers*
>
> *Educators don't have the answer.*
>
> *Where do we find the answer?*

First, we must realize and accept the fact that marriage is a Spiritual Institution and the answer will come through a spiritual source. The answer is in the Word of God: The Holy Bible. It's my belief that any problem we can have in this life, God Our Creator, has already given us the answers in the Bible. If we seek him diligently and with an open mind, He will reveal them to us. After seeking God and examining our teachings, I am convinced that they, for the most part, are good and with good intentions.

BUT, there are some important TRUTHS that are being left out of the teachings, such as:

a). Marriage is about ministry.

b). Marriage is made in heaven

c). Marriage is spiritual.

d). Marriage is God's doing.

e). Marriage is the basis for family structure.

f). Marriage is forever.

If we don't know these things, we will never understand the essence or significance of marriage.

Proverbs 18:22 "Whoso findeth a wife findeth a good thing." This scripture is being mis-interpreted in Christian churches all over these United States. Many Christian leaders are teaching their followers that a man can look for a wife, but a woman can't, look for a husband because the scripture said whoso findeth a wife, finds a good thing. It didn't say anything about a woman finding a husband; therefore a woman is not qualified to look for a husband. They tell the unmarred woman that she should wait until some man come along and discovers her. Let's Get Real: Neither woman nor man is qualified to find their spouse by natural means. The only way for anyone to look for their spouse is praying with hope. HOPE means honest expectation. EXPECTATION means to look for. Mark 11:24 "Therefore I say unto you, what thing soever ye desire, when ye pray, believe that ye receive them, and ye shall have them." You must look for whatever you pray for. That's faith. That works for man or woman.

To examine the first part of Proverb 18:22, let's take a little closer look. It says; if a man finds a wife he finds a good thing. It didn't say, if a man finds a woman to become his wife, it didn't say if a man finds a woman to marry and to make her his wife; neither did it say if a man finds a good woman. It didn't say if a man finds a saved woman, but if a man finds a wife (present tense). In this verse of scripture the word wife is not referring to a woman who is married, but to a woman that God has armed with special gifts and talents to be a wife. It refers to a woman who has allowed God to make her into a wife or wife material. It is the same for the man. He is a husband when God makes him into a husband.

God looks on the heart. I have been married to a wonderful woman for more than forty years now. When my wife, I call her Jean, took the marital vowels and said "I Do" she became my wife at that point. She became a wife indeed when God set his approval on her as a wife.

When God made us human beings, He made us different. He put different talents and gifts in each of us. Because we can't see into a person's heart, we don't know what gifts or talents are there until the gift or talent is manifested. God doesn't have to wait for a manifestation. He knows what gifts He has given us. God may look on a man who is a thief, drunkard or an adulterer, who has never been in a church and call him preacher. He called Gideon a mighty man of valor, (a brave warrior) when Gideon was a coward. The Bible says he was hiding behind some stuff. (Scared)

God said, "When a man find a wife he finds a good thing," God is referring to the special gift/s He has deposited in the hearts of some women to be a wife. Not all women are gifted to be wives. If you can't see the inside of another person's heart, I would suggest you close your eyes, walk in faith and let God choose your spouse;

He never misses the mark.

He is a perfect match-maker.

Marriages really are made in heaven.

Marriage is God's business.

Marriage is God's doings

Unity of Husband and Wife

Genesis chapter 2, God assigned man a great responsibility. He was given charge over all that God had created and made in the earth. Genesis 2:18 then God said, "It is not good that the man should be alone, I will make him a help meet..."

God gave Adam a wife to help him fulfill the ministry that had been assigned to him. Companionship, security, and sex are a few of the fringe benefits that come under the umbrella of marriage. When God brings two people together He is concerned about the ministry that He has designed for each of them. Every person has a ministry wherewith God has assigned them. This is one of the reasons He tells us, "Be ye not unequally yoked together with unbelievers." 2 Cor. 6:14.

The husband and wife cannot fully support one another in their ministry if one is serving God and the other is serving someone else. Amos 3:3 "Can two walk together, except they be agreed?" You don't want to marry someone that's not saved, someone that doesn't believe in God. It might be a good person, easy to get along with. It doesn't matter. If they are unbelievers they are off limit. Marriage is about ministry. God cannot use an unbeliever in his ministry. An unbeliever is an enemy to God. If a Christian is married to a sinner, they will have trouble trying to please each other. As a matter of fact it is impossible.

Marriages Are Made In Heaven

God told Israel not to marry anyone that was not a Jew. He is saying to his bride, the Christian; do not marry anyone that's not a Christian.

The Christian religion has many denominations. If Christians of different denominations want to get married, they should choose a denomination both can serve. The word married means togetherness. As it relates to ministry, it's better if the husband and wife are members of the same denomination, and yes the same church.

In marriage the husband and his wife should complement one another in their ministry. If you are in ministry you are also in warfare with Satan. Satan is always on his job trying to hinder ministry. The wife is to provide help and strength to the husband. Likewise the husband should bring strength and covering to his wife. You fight better together. One can chase a thousand, and two can put ten thousand to flight.

God wants us to develop a relationship with him early in life, and let him direct our lives. He is commanding us to yield our lives to him before choosing a career or getting married. Ecclesiastes 12:1 "Remember now thy creator in the days of thy youth." Matthew 6:33 "Seek ye first the kingdom of God, and his righteousness; and all these things shall be added onto you."

Most people try to plan their lives without God's help. Not realizing that they are not in charge of their lives. God gave us this commandment for a reason. The reason being, He has a purpose and a plan for each of us.

So many are guilty of doing just the opposite of what God commands. They get an education, a job or a career, get married and sometimes have children before turning to God and asking, Lord what do you want me to do? That's when they realize that the education they have acquired is in the wrong field to contribute to the ministry which they are called: The career they chose is actually a hindrance to the ministry. The spouse they have chosen, without God's help, simply does not fit in the ministry that God has planned for them. God's will is for the husband and wife to be a team serving together. God wants to save us in our youth when we are strong, when we can run, when we can fight. The old is for council. The young is for war.

When we leave God out of our plans, we are asking for trouble. When we leave Him out of our marriage we are headed for disaster. I like to think of a godly marriage as having three persons; the husband, the wife and the Lord. The Lord being the center, He never moves. He is the adhesive that holds married couple together. How many times have you heard this? The husband and wife grew apart so they are getting a divorce. Now you can tell them:

> *you cannot grow apart from*
>
> *each other without leaving Christ,*
>
> *because he is the center of the marriage.*

What they need to do is turn around, and draw near to Christ. When they are close to Christ again, they will be close to each other again. There is no reason for divorce.

Now concerning husbands and wives drifting apart; this is so serious. I'm seeing preachers and pastors, people in high places in the ministry being deceived. People who have been teaching and counseling others for years are now getting divorced. Their story is; we just grew apart, no one is at fault. No one is to be blamed, and we are still friends. #1 To say no one is at fault, is a lie straight from the Devil's house (hell). #2 Any time there is a divorce between two Christians somebody is at fault. #3 Someone is to be blamed, most of the time both parties are at fault. We will have to answer to God. Oh yes, He is holding somebody responsible. So they say, we're still friends. God doesn't bring two people together in holy matrimony and make them one flesh just to be friends. They were or should have been friends before marriage. God brings us together to be husband and wife. And His commandment is that we stay married until we are separated by death. Anybody that is qualified to be married already knows that they have a responsibility to protect their marriage, to keep the relationship strong. If you fail to work on your marriage, your marriage will fail, and you are at fault.

Yes, YOU are at fault. You are to be blamed. Some are saying we don't love each other anymore. They have to be referring to a romantic love. It's sad to know that many people are basing their marriage on romance. Romance is but a small component of what marriage is about. Commitment is a greater component.

Commitment says, I will always love you;

I will always be there for you...

I will always do you good and not evil as long as I live;

I will always be caring and forgiving toward you...

That's the marriage vow.

that's how God defines love.

As children of God we do not operate in man's love alone. We operate in God's love. God's love can't be turned on and off at will.

when the love of God

is in action in your life

you don't control it, it controls you.

You can't stop loving even if you want to. You can't stop loving even if the spouse does you wrong or leaves you. God is love, 1 Corinthians

13:4 says, "Love suffers long and is kind; love envieth not; love vaunteth not itself, is not puffed up, doth not behave itself unseemly…"

As long as you walk with God, you have love. You can only stop loving when you leave God. Something is badly wrong when two Christians get a divorce. Somebody somehow has missed God. To love one's spouse is not an option it is a command. Ephesians 5:25 reads, Husbands, love your wives, even as Christ also loved the church, and gave himself for it; Vs.28 So ought men to love their wives as their own bodies. He that loveth his wife loveth himself. Vs.33b Nevertheless let every one of you in particular so love his wife even as himself;… Colossians 3:19 Husbands, love your wives, and be not bitter against them.

God commands the husbands to love their wives. It seems strange He would say that, when He has already commanded us to love everybody even our enemy? He is not itemizing, or being repetitious. He is not speaking of love as an emotion or a strong feeling as Webster defines the word love.

He is using the word love as a verb, an action word. He is saying exemplify your love, do love, He said, "Love your wives and be not bitter toward her".

He made no exceptions. It doesn't matter what she has done, love her and forgive her. So we know that he is talking to Christians, men that are full of the Holy Ghost, possessing the love of God and the mind of Christ, having the ability to forgive, men that understand God's definition of the words love and forgiveness.

God's definition of the word forgiveness is, as though it never happened. When we sin against God and repent he puts it in the sea of forgetfulness and never remembers it again. The relationship is restored; there is no bitterness, it is as if it never happened. The Bible says we all have sin and we all do sin. God looks beyond our faults and sees our needs. Not only does He see our needs, but He stands all day with His arms reaching to us wanting to bless us, deliver us, and take care of our needs. The bible says, God has ten thousand blessings in his right hand to satisfy the poor.

Marriages Are Made In Heaven

Bobby L. Woods

COUNSELING

Counseling Before Marriage

Many people never seek counseling before marriage non-Christian and Christians alike. It's typical to hear of hurting couples seeking professional help once their marriage starts to fall apart. This is certainly not the best policy, but I do agree one should do everything within his/her power to save their marriage. God honors marriage even if the marriage starts without honoring God. Hebrews 13:4 Marriage is honorable in all, and the bed undefiled. Most Christian who go to their pastor or spiritual leader for premarital counseling already have their minds made up. Oftentimes they are already engaged. I'm told some have already set a wedding date before they go for counseling. Some have already moved in together. What do they want? What could they want from the preacher at this point? There is not much chance of him (the preacher) changing their minds. These couples are at the point of no return, without somebody getting hurt.

Who Is Qualified To Perform

Pre-Marital Counseling?

There are people who are educated in this area. They have degrees and are considered experts or professionals. These people earn a good living for themselves, getting paid a very high salary. But, if they are operating without God in their lives, they simply cannot understand the spiritual aspect of marriage. They are specialists, yet are unqualified for premarital counseling.

Psychology and Sociology gives one a general understanding of how people think and behave under various conditions and how people act and react in groups. These are very powerful sciences. Anyone who is intellectually empowered in these areas has a step up on the average person. Nevertheless, there is a spiritual side of marriage that human knowledge or education just can't touch.

Pastors are the best, or should be the best source for marital and premarital counseling. Anybody taking this position needs to have a close relationship with God. Some pastors are unqualified because they don't understand that marriage is spiritual as well as natural. Anyone who does not know that marriage is Spiritual, sacred, and about ministry, will not be able to properly and effectively minister in this area.

I am concerned about pastors who have more than one living wife. In my opinion, these ministers disqualify themselves according to, I Timothy 3:2 "A pastor then must be blameless, the husband of one wife. See also Titus 1:6.

How can a pastor expect others to follow his advice, or how can he give Bible based advice when he is living contrary to what the Bible says concerning pastors? I'm not saying that the pastor can't be saved having more than one living wife. I do believe it disqualifies him as a marriage counselor.

If the pastor got a divorce when he had marital problem how can he help me when I'm having problems in my marriage?

What can he say? Can he tell me to hang on, keep praying, God will help me work things out. Your action speaks louder than your words.

This reminds me of a pastor that lived in my community. He preached the Gospel, but he didn't want to live by it. He had some ungodly habits that everybody was aware of. That pastor didn't try to hide his sins, but when he preached he would say to his audience "Don't do as I do, but do as I say do." Believe it or not, this preacher had several followers. Apostle Paul said, "Follow me as I wholly follow Christ." If you don't live it, you're not qualified to teach it. Luke 6: 42 How canst thou say to thy brother, Brother let me pull out the mote that is in thine eye, when thou thyself beholdest not the beam that is in thine own eye?

In order to be an effective instructor you should not teach by precept only, but by precept and example.

Don't just tell me what should be done.

Don't just tell me how it should be done,

but prove to me that it can be done.

In other words, you do it first.

You must first be a partaker

Purpose For Pre– Marital Counseling

When a person decides to get married he/she is making one of the most important decisions they will ever make in life. Anybody contemplating marriage desperately needs someone holy, and with godly wisdom, to advise them. They need someone who has a close relationship and experience with God to coach them and not to make the decision for them. They need to pray and seek God with them and mirror the pros and cons that they might make the right decision.

People need premarital counseling because of an emotion called infatuation. Infatuation is so often mistaken for love. People are overwhelmed by something about another person, other than their personality, or the content of their character, which is who a person really is. For instance, some women are highly attracted to men that are superstars, sportsmen, and sometimes think they are really in love. Most often, they don't know or barely know the person. Men are attracted to women who are considered beautiful as the case of Samson in the Bible.

Marriages Are Made In Heaven

My definition for the word infatuation is; fool's love. It shines like love, it looks like love, it feels like love. It's just like love in many ways, but it is not strong enough to be a foundation for marriage. It won't stand when the serious problems of life come into the marriage. Problems will come. If a man is infatuated because of a woman's beauty, which is something about the woman, and mistakes it for love, what happens when wrinkles and extra pounds come and her beauty is gone? The simple answer to that question is, his love or what he thought was love is gone as well.

My daughter met a young man, a church goer. As a matter of fact, he was a preacher, handsome, good looking, a smooth talking preacher, who made all kinds of promises. This young man attended church on regular basis. He attended Sunday school and other Bible studies. He was quite respectful. He seemed to have had all of the qualities of a Christian, but he did not have the love of God. The love of God is one thing that cannot be duplicated. He didn't have that one quality that makes a Christian a Christian, the love of Christ, or the Spirit of God. My daughter disregarded that one important fact. She was swept off of her feet. She was infatuated.

She refused counseling or advice. She was sure that it was true love. She married this man, but as soon as she said "I Do" her very words were "It hit me, I just made a big mistake." Of course, this marriage didn't last. Knowing this was a mistake from the beginning left her defenseless, when the problems came. She had nothing to hold on to, nothing to fight with, no hope of saving the marriage. After one year and one child the marriage ended in divorce. I appreciate my daughter for allowing me to share her story. I'm hoping it will help someone else. Because, bizarre as her story may sound, it is not an isolated incident. It's happening all around us every day.

People who are about to get married need extensive counseling. Because when people fall in love or think they are in love, they have a tendency to close their eyes to what is real. They put all of their focus on what they feel. If all you have is what you feel, you don't have enough to build a marriage.

Premarital counseling is supposed to bring one back into reality. It is designed to bring all kinds of real life issues to the minds of the lovebirds; the good, the bad, and even the ugly. That they might make a conscious decision, and answer some important questions that should be in the back of every potential spouses mind, such as;

Are we ready for this?

Are we right for each other?

Is this the right time?

Is this God's will for me?

Will this person be a helper to my ministry?

Will they be a hinder to my ministry?

Will I be a helper or hinder to theirs?

God instituted marriage that two people (male and female of course) would be united in love, to be loyal, faithful, and committed helpers to one another in the ministry and otherwise. It doesn't matter if you are young or old; if you are planning on getting married you need counseling. Even if you have counseled others, when it's your time you need counseling too. It's not so easy for one to see their own shortcomings. It doesn't matter who you are, where you have been, what you know, or how many times you have been married before. If you are contemplating marriage please get counseling. You might be surprised what you learn about yourself.

SEX EDUCATION

Sex Before Marriage

Sex before marriage is called FORNICATION. The Bible teaches us that sex is for married people only. As Christians we must allow God to keep our minds pure because fornication and adultery are seriously dangerous sins. And they first take place in the mind. One doesn't have to actually commit the act to be considered guilty. Matthew 5:28 Jesus words; "Whosoever looketh on a woman to lust after her hath committed adultery with her already in his heart". Timothy warns his readers to flee from fornication. Parents are obligated to teach their children to honor their bodies, to keep themselves clean and free from sex until they are married.

We watch our boys and girls sneak around the church holding hands, touching, and even kissing. These kinds of things are happening in and around our churches. We say that is natural, today that's what teenagers do. Yes, it is what teenagers do. It's also the way teenagers get in trouble. We call it puppy love: Pastor Ozell Northern of Dayton Ohio often said from his pulpit, "Be careful with puppy love, it can lead to a dog's life." Another quote he often said to his church members; "Don't sow your wild oats and ask me to pray for a crop failure".

Sex before marriage is commonplace in our society today. It's not uncommon for a man or a woman to have slept around with twenty five or thirty sex partners before marriage. Thirty is a small number for the average man who lives as a bachelor until he is thirty years of age. For some people one hundred is a small number. Sexual intercourse is for married couples. And I did say couples! Not threesomes', foursomes none of that stuff. Not self-administered. And not from long distance on the telephone. (phone sex is taboo.) Sex is for one man and one woman, husband and his wife together. People that have made a life-time commitment to one another.

God designed sex to be something beautiful, something holy, something sacred. What our society has made sex to be is so far removed from what God designed it to be. There is no resemblance, and I believe we have reached the point of no return. God and only God can turn this thing around. What God designed to be good, holy and beautiful we, the people of this generation, have turned it into something ungodly and sinful. God is not pleased; He is getting weary of our wicked ways.

Dangers in Fornication

If people would think of the dangers of having sex outside of marriage, I do believe they would come to the conclusion that it's really not worth the risk. Risk #1 is you are taking a chance on losing your soul to hell's fire, because you are in disobedience to God's will. Risks #2 there are people, not a few, who change drastically after a sexual encounter. They appear to be very nice, friendly, peace loving people. After one sexual session, a possessive spirit takes them over. They are out of control, and very dangerous. They think they should be able to come to your house anytime of the day or night. Some will stalk you, and will hurt you or even kill you, if you try to be with someone else. Risk #3 STD's (sexually transmitted diseases). I believe that some of these deadly diseases we are experiencing today are plagues that God is allowing to come in among the people as He did back in the Bible days. Because the people were evil, stiff-necked and disobedient, God sent fiery serpents among the people. (read Numbers 21:5-6) Risk #4 child/children being conceived. There are a great number of men, good men, some are Christian wanting to get married and have families. The problem is they have children by other women. No woman wants to start a life with a man that has two or three children with other women. He might be a good, hardworking man but most of his earnings will go to other women, for child support. It's the same for women. Some men are acutely afraid to marry women with children. Others just don't want the responsible of raising another man's children. Some men are afraid of the biological dead beat father, especially those who walked off and left his children.

There has to be something short, something evil about him. Here is the problem the next man is afraid of. He is afraid that the first time he tries to discipline the child the biological deadbeat father will roll up or call up, laying down rules as how to, or how not to discipline HIS child or children. (the ones he walked off and left). Sometimes making threat's on the step parent life. These are just a few risks one encounters by being sexual active before marriage.

It's About Sex

People are getting married thinking that marriage is all about their physical needs and desires. Most of the time when you hear someone say, "I want to be married" or "I need to be married," they are thinking in terms of companionship, security or sex, yes, sex. Sex is usually at the top of the list. That applies to young and older saints and sinners. An older gentleman in our church announced he was going to get married. His son was concerned because his dad was eighty years old. The son asked, why do you want to get married? Are you looking for companionship or sex? His dad replied, "Both." Yes the old guy had sex on his mind.

When God gives one a spouse, he is thinking ministry. God is not overly concerned about our hormones or sexual drive. As a matter of fact, until we are over-comers in that area of our lives, we are not ready for marriage. There are Christian men and women, who are weak in this area, which has not been able to keep themselves. These people are getting married thinking they can live a godly life if they have a spouse to take care of their sexual desires. That's false hope. The truth is, if you can't live saved single, you won't be able to stay saved married. Only God can save, and only God can keep you saved. If you are taken by an adulterous spirit, marriage won't save you. You need to be delivered from that spirit. You need to understand before getting married, that marriage is no guarantee that sex will always or ever be available for you, even though you are married. Something could happen to the spouse or you between the bridal room and the bedroom that could render you unable to fulfill the sexual duty. Of course, I know this is highly unlikely, but possible. The point is, sex alone is not a good enough reason for marriage.

Adultery is a spirit; you can't satisfy it. You must overcome it. You may have a spouse and a sweetheart too, but if you are plagued with an adulterous spirit you will not be satisfied. You can never please an adulterous spirit. King Solomon had seven hundred wives and three hundred concubines. That's one thousand women. I'm sure that was more than enough women to take care of his sexual needs. Don't you think? Yet he was not satisfied. Of course everyone knows or should know that once you step into the cheating arena, you are opening yourself up to all kinds of evil. Anyone taking this route should know that they are leaving God's instruction and covering. They are taking matters in their own hands. No good results can come out of this. Not ever!

King David (Solomon's father) had wives & concubines. Yet, 2 Samuel

11:2 says, And it came to pass in an evening tide, that David arose from off his bed, and walked upon the roof of the King's house: and from the roof he saw a woman washing herself; she just happened to be the wife of Uriah. He was one of David's best friends, a captain in his army. This woman was very beautiful to look upon. Her name was Bathsheba. David, being overwhelmed by lust and an adulterous spirit, thought he had to have her. So he murdered his friend and took his wife. David did not need another wife by any means; he was not trying to fulfill a need but a lust. This woman was the mother of King Solomon. Again I say one cannot satisfy a lustful spirit. Lust is sin, it brings death. It will cause you to destroy others and yourself.

David married this woman hoping to live happily ever after. It didn't work out quite the way he wanted. Because of that marriage King David suffered greatly. He spent many nights without sleep, went days without food, (fasting). He lost relationships with friends, family members, and with God. This is only a part of the pain, suffering, heart break, hurt, and shame that came upon David because of this relationship. God spoke to David through the prophet Nathan 2 Samuel 12: 8a I gave thy master's house, and thy master's wives into thy bosom, and gave thee the house of Israel and of Judah; Vs. 9a Wherefore has thou despised the commandments of the LORD, to do evil in his sight? Thou hast killed Uriah the Hittite with the sword, and taken his wife to be thy wife, and hast slain him with the sword of the children of Ammon. Now therefore the sword shall never depart from thine house; because thou hast despised me, and hast taken the wife of Uriah the

Hittite to be thy wife. Vs. 11 Thus saith the LORD, Behold I will raise up evil against thee out of thine own house, and I will take thy wives before thine eyes, and give them unto thy neighbor, and he shall lie with thy wives in the sight of this sun. Vs. 12 For thou didst it secretly but I will do this thing before all Israel, and before the sun.

They Call It Sex

In a marital relationship, the husband and wife should seek to satisfy each other in every way, especially in the bedroom. Many of our brothers are a little dumb in this area. They don't realize that. All they know is to satisfy themselves. I heard a brother say, "We start at the same time, if she doesn't finish it is her fault." I have been told there are women who live with men for years, having sexual intercourse often, but never or hardly ever reach a climax. The brother doesn't know this. He does his thing and come away thinking he had just rocked her world. But in reality, he had just disappointed her again, and left her feeling not satisfied but unfulfilled. This should not be. And it doesn't have to be. It's for the most part the result of poor communication. In order to have a healthy marriage and a healthy sex life there must be communication. For some reason women won't tell their husbands when they fail to satisfy them in the bedroom. They have no problem telling them when they are pleased. When they are not pleased they would rather fake it than tell the truth. There are women who go outside of the marriage and become sexually involved with other men, (adultery) not for the sakes of having sex. They love their husbands and want to stay married to him, but they are not being fulfilled sexually. These women are actually cheating to save their marriage. They are committing adultery trying to get the monkey off of her back. (So to speak)

Hebrews 13:4a says, Marriage is honorable in all, and the bed undefiled...

Some Christians believe and teach that anything goes in the bedroom of a married couple. What they don't seem to understand is that they belong to God. Nothing is hidden from Him. He can see what goes on in the privacy of the bedroom. Some are teaching that it's okay to bring in sex toys, tools and mechanical devices. God forbid!

I walked into a bookstore, thinking it was a regular book store. Once inside I realized that it was not a regular bookstore but an adult bookstore. The place was full from wall to wall, with all kinds of so called sex tools and toys. Some stuff I had never seen and never want to see again. I saw whips, ropes, dancing poles, handcuffs, vibrators, false penises, different sizes, shapes and colors. I saw every ungodly thing that you could imagine.

I could sense a bad spirit in that place. I was ashamed to come out. A

Christian can't be in a place like that without feeling condemned. How can they use this stuff and not be shamed? Plus, I keep hearing in the news of someone being killed or dying using these toys or being involved in some ungodly sex act. It is my belief concerning sex tools and toys, and mechanical devices, anybody using that kind of equipment in their bedroom is not having sex. I don't know what to call it, but it's not sex. It sounds a little creepy and destructive. This generation is sex crazy. Yes crazy! Men and women are meeting and sleeping together on the same day and the same hour. They don't even know each other's first name! This is simply crazy.

If you are in the top of your teenage years and are not sexually active, people will think something is wrong with you. Adult Christians don't help the matter. I'll give you an example. If we ask a young girl how old are you? If she says 15, 16, 17 we ask, do you have a boyfriend? If she says no, we ask why not? And make a dumb statement like; a pretty girl like you doesn't have a boyfriend? What should be said to her is, "That's good, and you'll have plenty of time for boyfriends and dating. Get your mind on completing your education, and seeking the will of God for your life.

A great number of these young sex crazy men of this generation rate sex as the most important thing in the world next to life itself. These men think they should have two or three sexually active girlfriends just to be assured of not ever having to go lacking in case one or two of them are not able to perform at any given time.

Solomon was known as the smartest man in the world. He was a great King and a great judge. Yet concerning women, the man was CRAZY. He had one thousand women that he could have any time any day, or night. He had more money than he could spend. He was really living big. One day He woke up and said, "This is CRAZY," (These are my words). Solomon declared it was all vanity and vexation of spirit. Now I know if we do not apply the God factor in every aspect of our lives it is all in vain. I have learned over the years that no man can fully realize the definition of sex apart from a monogamous commitment. It doesn't matter how many women a man has or have had, or how long he has been sexually active, when he makes the monogamous commitment his sexual experience will elevate to another level.

I know sex is spiritual. That is to say God has a part in it. Yes God is a part of what goes on in our bedroom. When we put sexual tools and toys in our bedrooms we are putting God out. Anything that replaces God in any area of our lives is demonic.

What is sexual intercourse? (penetration, workout and ejaculation) is how most young people and some old ones as well define sex. (That's it.). Sexual intercourse is only a part of the sexual experience. If all we know about sex is intercourse (penetration, workout and ejaculation) we don't know very much. We are missing the blessings that God has designed for married couples in the sex plan. It's a packaged deal and He wants us to have the whole package. I'm not a sex expert by any means, but I'm so excited about the little that I do know. I want to share it.

I learned it from the Bible

I know that God made sex.

I know that sex is spiritual.

I know that sex is for reproduction.

I know that it is for the husband and the wife's pleasure.

I know that through sex the couple ministers to one another.

I know that in the sexual experience

penetration should not be the beginning

and ejaculation doesn't have to be the end.

The question that I have struggled with is, If God made sex for our enjoyment and to bless us in ministry; why does it have to end for most men long before their lives end? It is a good thing, so why did he not make it a life time thing? As I sought the answer to this question, the thought came to me that sex was designed to be a blessing to the married couple for a life-time; and it will if you know the full scope of the sexual experience. You have to know that sex is more than mere intercourse. (penetration, workout and ejaculation).

Sex In Three Dimensions

I was encouraged with the thought of sex as having three dimensions:

Dimension I.

This dimension consists of penetration, workout and ejaculation. There's no foreplay and nothing after, just wham-bam thank you mam. For most young people and some not so young, this is the totality of the sexual experience. They start the session with their minds set on the end. The only focus is the few seconds of explosive pleasure at the end of the work-out. When that happens, that's all there is to it. They are finished. It's cigarette time, so to speak.

Dimension II.

Is when the man and his wife come together taking time for foreplay...expressing their love for one another by touching, hugging, or whatever, communicating etc., etc; causing their emotions and imaginations to run wild. This couple is doing the things that should be done before penetration. They are doing the right things but with the wrong mindset. From the beginning and even before the beginning to the ending their main focus is on the last few seconds of pleasure because that is the part of the experience that we recognize as end of sex.

Dimension III.

Is the husband and wife committing for the most part the same action as in #2, but with a total different mindset. It should start with a courting session. What I call a courting session is when two people who are attracted to one another, in this case, husband and wife, delegate time to communicate and express their feelings toward one another. They are focusing on being together….touching and giving themselves to each other and being touched in a sexual manner.

Because there is communication, each party (the husband and wife) knows how to minister to one another sexually. Song of Solomon 2:6 His left hand is under my head and his right hand doth embrace me. This is called foreplay, but in #3 we can't call it foreplay. The word foreplay implies that there is something else coming after the play time which would be the main focus. In #3 there may or may not be anything to come after playtime. You might want to lie in one another's arms holding and caressing one another for the sake of holding and caressing, or just cuddling raw (nude). They are not focusing on what might happen in the last few seconds as in dimensions 1 & 2. They are focusing on every aspect of the play time, whether hugging, caressing or whatever. Your focus is on these things; itemized, if caressing enjoy that….hugging, focus on that, and not on a thrill that might come at the end. Song of Solomon 1:13b Solomon tried to help when he said "He will lie all night betwixt my breasts". You should be enjoying and making the best of everything as you perform it. If the process should progress to that few second thrill at the top of blueberry hill that will be wonderful: but if it doesn't that's all good too. You have enjoyed much of the physical side of the sexual experience, and have allowed the gender spirits (male and female) to minister to each other; to the soul and flesh of the two of you.

This is the sexual experience that God ordained.

This is an experience to be proud of.

This is an experience that God is a part of.

This experience can last a lifetime.

This experience is a gift from God.

Sex is spiritual as well as physical. It is designed to temporally take you above life situations. It takes you to a place in the spirit where trials and troubles of this world can't touch you. At the same time it is refreshing and strengthening you and much more. The sexual experience is awesome. In my opinion you can never be closer to Heaven (alive) than you are when in a godly sexual experience. 'A bit of humor.'

Dimensions 1 and 2 main focus is on the few second thrill at the end of the session. The problem with that is when age or illness makes that part impossible; you have nothing to reach for. You have no reasons for play time, which is known as foreplay. Foreplay has no purpose if there nothing after. With that mind-set one will miss out on the blessed part of the sexual experience. This is just a part of what sex is about.

> sex brings gratification to the flesh
>
> marriage should bring glorification to god;
>
> marriage is about ministry.
>
> Marriage is Spiritual and so is sex!

Sex For Seniors

For older people setting dates for sex might not be a good thing. For instance, when we were young, with children in the house and working different shifts, we might set a date for Thursday night. If the opportunity comes open on Wednesday we might just pass. We know Thursday night is coming soon. We are in ours seventh's now and every time we wait for a set date something comes up or one is called away or one or both of us start hurting somewhere in our bodies. Sometimes it seems as though I'm having pain everywhere.

When you reach seventy you might get pains in places you didn't think one could have pains. Like under your chin, on top of the foot, in between your fingers, in your little toe, at the back side of your neck, even under your fingernail. My wife used to get these headaches. Now both of us get headaches. It goes like this, she'll say, "Honey I haven't forgotten what we talked about but, I have a headache." I'll whisper this little praise, "Thank you God! I've got a headache too". Excuse my humor I'm a little silly today. Take this little cliché seriously; forget appointments, when ability and opportunity meet, let it happen. That's the real deal. AWAY WITH SETTING SEX DATES.

Bobby L. Woods

WHY MARRIAGES FAIL

Marriages fail because people take it upon themselves to find and to choose their spouses. That is really not man's privilege; because, no man is qualified to find the right spouse to aid him in his ministry without the leading of the Lord. Every person that's called to be married, I do believe, God has a special mate for them. But when one chooses another mate, other than the one that God has designed, it will be harder to make that marriage work. It's like trying to fit a square peg into a round hole. The only way to make it fit is to trim off the corners of the peg which should not be. So it is when one chooses a spouse without God's leading. They will undoubtedly suffer and go though some things that should not be.

Becoming Too Common

The husband and his wife are friends, and they should be the best of friends. The person you marry should be considered your best friend. But always be careful that you never take your spouse for granted. And don't become too common with one another. For instance some men like to see their wives in the nude. But if she goes around the house naked from day to day, it will soon take the edge off of the excitement. Never get so common that you disregard hygiene. Most women know this, but men sometimes forget. It has been said that women like to smell their man being a little musty after a day of work. They are being proud to have a working man. That is so untrue. Work or no work stink is stink! Nobody enjoys smelling the stench of another person's body.

Unwashed bodies will smell.

Some men like to get their baths in the morning. They say it helps get them awake and going. Think about this, if you only clean up before you go off to work, the only time you spend at home with the wife you smell like work. You stink! Don't even think about going to bed without washing your body. Nobody wants to touch, cuddle or have any sexual action with someone that is unclean. As a matter of fact, it's just disrespectful to get under the same sheets with anybody being unwashed. The more a woman has to smell her husband's stench, the more she enjoys smelling other men who smell good. Wives should keep themselves clean, smelling good, looking good and above all create a luxurious atmosphere in the bedroom.

The seventh chapter of Proverb tells the story of a married woman who decided to play the harlot while her husband was out of town. She found a man that she wanted to be with and asked him to come home with her. The young man knew that was wrong. She persuaded him by telling him that her house, her bedroom, and her bed were clean, sprayed with perfume, and smelling good. All I'm trying say is; without good hygiene habits none of the above will work. Too disregard good hygiene practices is being much too common!

I said earlier that sex is spiritual. It's more sacred than I can explain. When engaged in sexual intercourse you are giving a part of yourself to another person. And it's something you can never get back. The Bible says in sexual intercourse, the two become a part of one another. That's a spiritual connection, any way you look at it.

I Corinthians 6:15 &16 says ...Your bodies are members of Christ, shall I then take the members of Christ, and make them the members of an harlot? God forbid. Vs. 16 What? Know ye not that he which is joined to an harlot is one body? For two, said he, shall be one flesh.

I think maybe that's one reason why so many marriages fail. Too many people have become a part of too many other people, by having sexual intercourse before they get married. The adjustment is all but impossible. Just know that sex is more serious than the average person, spiritual or non-spiritual, can perceive. Sex is sacred; it's not just for fun. Sex outside of marriage can cause very serious and negative repercussions. I Corinthians 6:18b says, Every sin that a man doeth is without the body; but he that committed fornication sinneth against his own body.

Lying

Lying to one another, don't start it.! Lying to one's spouse is one of the worst things a married person can do. A lie cannot support itself. When you tell one lie, you can get ready because chances are you'll have to tell another one to cover the first one, and so on. The truth will come out sooner or later. The lie will be uncovered and trust will be destroyed.

To be in a marriage without trust is a painful place to be. Telling the truth is always the best policy, even when it hurts. I've heard people say "I had to tell a little lie for peace sake. Or I lied to keep from hurting someone else." I've used these excuses myself, before I became a Christian, of course.

The fact that one feels a need to lie is evidence that somebody has already lied or acted outside of the truth and now needs a cover. You don't always have to tell a lie to be a liar. Acting a lie is just as bad as telling a lie. Lying is of the devil. The Bible says Satan is a liar, and he is the father of lies. John 8:44

If you cover it up, sooner or later it will come up again. If a person is about to get married and have some ugly skeletons in their closet, the best thing they can do is come clean. Just come clean. If your spouse to be can't adapt to you as you really are, that's a good sign that this is not the right person for you to marry. God hates a lie, Ps. 101:7 He that telleth lies shall not tarry in his sight.

If they start out lying and hiding the truth, it won't be long before the situation will go from telling lies to living a lie. Walk in truth, Jesus is truth. John 8:32 "...Know the truth and the truth shall make you free."

When a person lies to their spouse they are setting themselves up for a failed marriage.

Marriages fail because people change after the newness wears off. The things we do to impress one another before we get married and shortly after stops, I'm speaking of the little things that show love, respect and honor such as; the husband opening the car door, holding the door when going into a building, the wife running his bath water, calling one another from work, making time for one another.

After a few months into the marriage, we seem to take the attitude that I don't have to do all of that stuff anymore. I've GOT YA Now. I can go back to being my real self.

That's cheating. That's breaking the rule. An old man told me before I got married about an unwritten rule that says "you should start out the way you can hold out". An old woman gave me rule No.2 She said "the same things it takes to get a wife is the same things it will take to keep her".

Comparison, That's a 'No, No'

Brothers, there is never a good time or occasion to compare your wife to another woman. Unless in your comparison you are making her better than the person that you are comparing her to. Don't even compare her to her own mother. Please don't compare her to your mother. If it is possible don't use the comparison card at all. I can tell you by experience, that's a very sensitive area. Everyone knows that regardless of how well you can do anything there is someone, somewhere, that can do that same thing better. However, there seems to be an unseen, unspoken, and unwritten law that says, once you are married you are obligated to make your spouse think that you believe there is no one anywhere who can be compared to her in anyway.

That's a law. If you break it, you might be in the dog house for a very long time. This (sin) is not easily forgotten or forgiven. It applies to the wife and the husband as well. This is one area where the husband is a little more sensitive than the wife. It destroys his ego. I promise you my sister; you don't want to go there. The brother will be referring to that incident for years to come. The Bible tells us that we should build one another up continually with words and deeds. Wives remember, being a Christian woman you have the power of life and death in your tongue. Proverb 14:1. Every wise woman buildeth her house: but the foolish plucketh it down.

Always be careful what you say to your spouse

once a thing is spoken, it is spoken,

you can't take it back.

Baggage From A Previous Marriage

It takes work, a lot of work, to make any marriage work under normal circumstances. But when the participant comes in bearing baggage from a previous marriage, this marriage is in trouble before it gets started. Divorcees must remember it takes time to heal from the hurt of a previous marriage. It takes more time for some than others. Anyone who has been married before and wants to marry again should give themselves time to heal. Not only should they give themselves healing time before remarrying; but, they should give themselves time to heal before getting into a relationship with another person.

By the same token, anyone who's considering marriage to a person who has recently lost a spouse, whether to death or divorce, should be careful to give that grieving person time to recover. Remember, you can't replace another person. You don't want to try and pick up the pieces of a broken heart and put it back together again. Give that person time to heal and to be whole again. Know this my sister\brother divorce hurts and hurting people have a tendency to hurt other people. Any man or woman who has gone through divorce and not be hurt is probably someone you would not want to be involved with. It seems that a person who has been married before would be easy to stay married to, because of their experience. But it's just the opposite. People who have experience a failed marriage, for the most part, start the next marriage with the baggage of the fear of failure. They are not able to trust again and have an unreal expectation that causes their spouse to be uncomfortable in the relationship.

According to statistics, a second marriage has only a 25% chance of survival. Twenty five percent is all you have to start your marriage with. Paul teaches us in 1 Corinthians 7:10-11 If there is a separation, one should not go out and marry someone else, but wait for God to save that spouse and be reconciled.

Emotional wounds always require time to heal. There is no substitute for time. Medicine won't fix the problem. Some people turn to self-medicating (drugs) which usually makes things worse. Some turn to food and end up with health problems. Some go into a promiscuous lifestyle and do a lot of craziness, trying to fix the problem. I must tell you nothing can heal a broken heart but time.

When someone is suffering from a broken heart, seemingly what they need is to enter a relationship right away with someone who cares about them. Someone who can help them get through the night, so to speak (Their time of hurting and healing). The hard truth is this is one mile the hurting spouse should walk along.

Too often, hurting spouses enter into a relationship with someone else to help them get through their time of grieving. The problem comes once they are healed. After the hurting subsides, once they can see clearly is when they begin to realize that this person who has served as a crutch for them to lean on during their time of pain, during their time of grief is really not who they want to be in a relationship with. The only true antidote for a broken heart is time and prayer. Don't deceive yourself. When you have loved and lost, whether it's to death or divorce, you are in a hurting place. You just have to deal with the reality of the situation. Seek the Lord for strength, and He will help you get through it. You can't replace a loved one with another person. This is a mistake that many young and some older Christian have made. You won't have to experience this hurt and suffering, if you are smart enough to learn from others mistakes.

Un-forgiveness

Un-forgiveness is tricky baggage. If you don't forgive your former spouse it will certainly have a negative effect on the next. I said it is tricky because if you ever forgive the former spouse, and you should, you just might realize you didn't need a divorce in the first place. Therefore you don't need a second spouse. You just need to get back together and live happily ever after.

A great percentage of people who have gone through divorce have regrets. After some time has passed, they forgive the former spouse. A small percentage will go back together. Most of the time, it will be too late. One or both parties will have gotten involved, or married someone else.

Once forgiveness takes place, they start remembering the good times and loving times they had together. Now you are not quite satisfied with the new husband/wife because you want to be with the old one. Some start sneaking around together. That's one reason second marriage survivor rates are low. It's almost impossible to have a happy healthy second marriage. It is God's will for us to be committed to make the first one work.

'What God has joined together let no man put asunder'

Overly Protective

A person who has been hurt in a first marriage often makes the mistake of holding back in the second marriage; they fear being hurt again, sometimes without realizing it. They want to love again, and they want to take the big step again. But, they want to protect their emotions from being hurt again. That's baggage. In order to have a successful marriage, both parties must be willing to give themselves totally and completely to one another. You will have to take the risk of being hurt again. Until you reach this point you are not ready for a second marriage.

After a failed marriage it might take a long time to get to this point.

Some never get there. But it is the requirement for a successful second marriage. That is the bottom line.

Some will follow their heart, and disregard this requirement. Go on and get married again, when they are not healed from the first marriage. They are setting themselves up for another failed marriage. This is why statics only give a second marriage a 25% chance of survival.

Marriages With Step - Children

A Blended Family

There was a time when rearing stepchildren was the same as raising biological children. I am afraid it's not quite that simple anymore. Satan is working full time and overtime making trouble in this area. Men are afraid to marry women with children and rightfully so. There are men whose lives have been destroyed or their reputations ruined. Some end up in prison trying to be a good step-father.

Children are smart now. If they are not pleased with a step parent or a parent, as far as that goes. They know that all they have to do is dial 911 and accuse that parent of abuse. That parent is in trouble. Sometimes, a child will concoct a story, and it is their word against the stepparent or parent. Anyone going into marriage where step-children are involved needs to know without any doubt that this union is ordained by God. If God puts his approval on the relationship, it will work. It doesn't matter what it looks like or what anybody thinks, says or does. If God gives a go signal, it will work.

The child abuse laws are critical but necessary because so many children are being abused and even molested by step parents and parents. The thought of being accused of abuse is not the only problem that many step-parents are facing. Sometimes, the step-parent and the children can't seem to bond. Sometimes, the child cannot accept another person being there trying to take the place of that missing parent. So they respond by rebelling usually against both the parent and the step-parent. Mothers be very careful in situations of this kind. Always remember, if you have young children, you have to put the children's needs before your own. This is a hard saying but until the man that you are interested in wins the hearts of your young children, he should not be able to win your hand in marriage. Never start a marriage where young children are involved unless there is love, honor and respect in action among all; parent, step-parent and children.

There are women who decide to get married with or without their children's approval. They set their children down and tell them, (something on this wise) "I'm in love with this man, and he is in love with me. We are getting married and you will have to get used to it." This is what I call the hard line approach. Many are doing this. But it's a very dangerous road to take. If a child is jealous, thinking the stepfather is trying to take their father's place, if there is hatred or if they have fear toward that man, this is a very dangerous situation to put a child in. Some children are being destroyed because of situations such as these. Some will come through okay, but some won't. Just remember mothers, you are responsible for the welfare of your children.

There are many things to be considered with blending families, especially when each of them has children. Both parents should be acquainted with one another's children. Age and sex of all children must be considered. Methods of discipline should be discussed and agreed upon before marriage. All children will need discipline, and some more than others. If one parent believes in using the rod or spanking his\her children and the other doesn't this a disaster waiting to happen. If two children are guilty of the same mischief, and you spank one and discipline the other one some other way; this won't work for long. The child will perceive that as you are being partial.

If a brother marries a woman with very young children, he will probably never experience the old (you are not my daddy) problem. You can win a young child's love by loving him/her. You don't need to spoil young children by giving them things they don't need and you can't afford, or by letting them off when they should be disciplined. Just love them for real, and be good to their mother. You will never win a child's love if he/she thinks you are being mean or disrespectful to their mom.

Mothers with small children, make sure that the man you are thinking about marrying is the kind of man who will love your children, and raise your children as his own before you say; "I Do".

Remember, if you have children you must

put the welfare of the children before your own.

Raising children is serious. Marriage is serious.

Don't try either one without God's help and directions.

With God all things are possible.

Secrets and Surprises

Financial status, debts, loans, and properties owned should all be discussed. Everything you own, everything you owe, everything you are, and everything you plan to be, should be discussed before marriage. Nothing held back, nothing hidden, nothing covered. Let it all hang out.

A healthy working relationship should be operative between you, your child/children, and the other biological parent before marriage is considered. The truth is; blending families will not be easy. But if both parties are open and truthful, and God is included it can work, and work successfully.

If you are a single parent and you've just read this chapter, it may have

Marriages Are Made In Heaven

put a little fear in your heart. You don't have to be afraid. What you have to do is trust God. It's a must! Give yourself, your children, and the entire situation over to God. He has never failed anyone who trusted in him. What is impossible for man is easy for God. He specializes in things that seem impossible.

THE GOD ORDAINED MARRIAGE

Genesis 2:24 states, *"Therefore shall a man leave his father and his mother, and shall cleave to his wife; and they shall be one flesh."*

Marriage Is For Grown - Ups

and

It's Forever

I say marriage is for grown-ups because it is such an important step. I'm not saying a person has to be twenty-one or any particular age before they can get married. What I am saying is one need to be mature. Because when someone gets married, it should be a lifetime commitment. In my opinion, children should not have to make that decision. However, I have known teen marriages to survive. Even though they were young they were mature and committed enough to handle it. By the same token, I've known some thirty and forty year olds who were not mature enough and the marriage fell apart under pressure. Marriage is not so easy after the newness wears off, and people get hurt. The key factors are; maturity, being led by God, and being willing to give and forgive (committed). Anybody who is not mature enough to make a lifetime commitment, or close enough to God to get his directions probably should forget marriage and find themselves a hobby. Marriage is not a play thing. It's not something you should take lightly. When you step into marriage, you step into the arena of responsibility and it AIN'T FOR KIDS. Pardon my grammar, but it's no play thing.

Marriage is serious,

it's spiritual, it's about ministry,

It's for grown-ups, and yes, It's for keep.

Think it out, Figure it out,

Talk it out, Pray it out,

Before you start walking it out.

Once you are married it's a life time trip. You can't wake up one day and say, O' I think I made a mistake. I'll go back to the judge and undo the whole thing. The marriage ceremony is a holy ceremony, meaning God is involved and he says let no man separate you.

I know a man who had been married three or four times. His take on the subject was, if the first marriage doesn't work just keep doing it until you get it right. This was a smart man but he didn't have a clue of what marriage was about. There are men and women who have been married for many years. Some have been married several times and yet they don't understand the essence of the marriage contract. So they use the method of trial and error (keep trying something until you get it right)

Christians cannot use the world's methods. If God is to be involved, he has to be in charge. Matthew 19:3-4, the Pharisees wanted to know on what grounds a man can divorce his wife. Vs. 5-6, Jesus told them, in the beginning God made them one, and declared that they would be no more twain but one flesh. Then he said, what God has joined together let nobody put asunder. He said in so many words there are no grounds for a man to put away his wife. Then he made one exception. He said, except it be for fornication. Jesus told them if you put away your wife for any other reason and marry another woman you commit adultery.

SAME SEX MARRIAGE

I don't believe there is any such thing as a same sex marriage. You might ask how I can say that there is no such thing as a same sex marriage, or you might ask, what the basis for this statement is. When in California, New York, and some other states men are marrying men and women are marrying women every day?

I make this statement because I am convinced that marriages are made in heaven, and I cannot find anywhere in the Bible where God ordains same sex marriages. Hebrews 13:4 says, marriage is honorable in all, and the bed undefiled. Where is the honor when two men or two women share a bed together as husband and husband or wife and wife? I see no honor. I see a bed defiled. I see a confuse mind being controlled by a demonic spirit. God does not choose one man for another man or one woman for another woman. I find this union to be unholy. It is not sacred. It is sinful, and it is not two people being made one. It is an abomination according to the Bible. God does not consider this union as marriage, and I don't either. There is no such thing as husband and husband or wife and wife. I believe these are two people lost in their sinful emotions. What they need is what all sinners need... that is salvation. One might say they didn't choose to be that way, or they were born that way. There are boys born with female characteristics and girls born with male characteristics. Yet, I believe to be gay is a choice they make. No one is born gay. No one is born perfect.

In Acts3:2 there was the lame man who was lame from his mother's womb. In John 9:1 a man was blind from his birth. Jesus healed both of them. We were all born in sin. We were all born messed up. That is why Jesus gave his life that we can be born again. I have no hatred for people of the gay community. As a matter of fact, the people that I know of the gay community are good people. I have family members, whom I love dearly, who are confused concerning their sexual identity. For the most part, I find most of the gay community, to be kind, gentle and considerate people.

For some reason, they seem to be more gifted than the average person and quick to learn. Nevertheless, according to the Bible, to practice a homosexual lifestyle is sin. I also believe that most homosexuals know that it's wrong, but they feel trapped with no way out. It is a stronghold, but there is a way out. Jesus is the way out. When you have tried everything and all has failed turn to Jesus. He can save anybody from anything. Nothing is too hard for God. God worked miracles back in the Bible days, and he is working miracles now. Hebrews 13:8 "Jesus Christ is the same yesterday, today, and forever."

Getting back to California, New York and those other states that are issuing licenses for same sex marriages; it's not only California, New York and a few other States anymore. It's all fifty States in America. Since I started writing this book Our highest authority, the Supreme Court have passed a law commanding all states of the U.S to issue marriage license to gay people. This is just another incidence where our lawmakers are legalizing sin.

Things change and people change, but my God never changes. Same sex marriage will never be right or permitted by God. It's just wrong!

Definition for the Word Marriage

According to Nelson's Illustrated Bible Dictionary, marriage is the union of a man and a woman as husband and wife. This union becomes the foundation for a family. Nelson goes on to tell the origin of marriage—Marriage was instituted by God when he declared, "It is not good that the man should be alone: I will make him a helper comparable to him" Genesis 2:18. So God fashioned woman and brought her to man.

Webster's New World Dictionary says; Marriage is being husband and wife.

WORLD BOOK ENCYCLOPEDIA- Marriage is the relationship between a man and a woman who have made a legal agreement to live together. When a man and a woman marry, they become husband and wife. Marriage is an important religious ceremony in many of the world's religions. Marriage is a strong institution. God used the word marriage to describe his relationship with the Church. Under the marriage institution He says to the Church, I will never leave you, nor forsake you, even onto the end of the world!

I get my information concerning marriage from books. beginning with the Bible, all of my books say

> *marriage is between a man and a woman.*
>
> *How much further down will we go?*

I'm old school. This homosexual (unisex) marriage thing must be in some new books that I'm not aware of yet. According to the Bible, the book that will never be outdated; God is very much a part of marriage. But in a marriage between two people of the same sex I can't find a space where God can fit in. Same sex marriage IS NOT a God thing. That is why I say, there is no such thing.

Marriages Are Made In Heaven

President Obama is a good president He did some good things for this country. But I did not agree with him when he endorsed same sex marriage. I was shocked! Bewildered! Why did he do that? I still don't agree with him on that issue. Even though, now I think I know why he did it. It was not a heart move, but a political move. If he had not endorsed that bill, he probably would not have worn the second term presidential election. I had no idea that there were so many gay people in our society. When the President signed that bill it was like he opened a flood gate. Homosexuals are showing up in every walk of life with no shame. We have doctors, educators, lawyers, entertainers, construction workers, food handlers, sport players even football players and more. Businessmen and men who have been married for several years are having relationship with other men on the DOWNLOW. Now they are coming out.

For some reason, I have always envisioned gay men as being small framed, timid, easygoing and good-looking. We called them pretty boys. I have never been more wrong! They come in every form, shape, colors, races, religions and nationalities. I have friends and relatives that I love, whom I thought were straight. Now that I know they are gay doesn't change my feeling toward them. I still love them. They are still my friends, but I can never agree to a gay lifestyle. It is not God's will for anyone

Our God Can Break Generational Curses

Children whose parents are separated or divorced have a tendency to blame themselves for their parents separating. All children, and I mean, all children, who fall victim to parental separation are scarred deeply. A great percentage of these victims never fully recover. I think it's safe to say that most of these never fully recover. Some grow up to be good people and never realize that they have a problem. They look normal, act normal, and believe themselves to be normal until they are adults and have children of their own. Then they find themselves being abusive or treating their children in some hurtful or evil way. This is the result of being a victim of abusive behavior. (Generational curse).

There are people spending time in prisons for hurting children, and they don't know what happened to them. They don't understand why they did what they did. There is a proverb that says, 'hurt people, hurt people'. This is just one of the things, or one problem that divorces produce.

If you are a victim of a broken home or parental separation know this. There is hope. GOD CAN AND WILL BREAK GENARATIONAL CURSES!

I'm just trying to wake some men up. Brothers please, please don't leave your children. I know, if parents realized how divorces affect children they would try a little harder to make their marriages work. It seems that too many parents don't understand that divorce leaves the children open for all types of problems; physically, emotionally, spiritually and otherwise.

Divorce is not a part of God's plan for his people. Divorce should not happen to God's people. Divorce is often detrimental for children. Children are not designed to handle divorce. Some children never overcome the negative side effects.

Divorce destroys children

Divorce destroys people

Divorce destroys homes

Divorce is an evil thing

Divorce is Satan's tool

God is a deliverer

God is a generational curse breaker

Remember!

Marriages are made in Heaven

Marriage is God's Doings

Marriage is the basis for Family Structure

Marriage is Sacred

Marriage is Spiritual

Marriage is about Ministry

Marriage is for Mature Adults

Be Alert

Watch for little foxes or they will destroy the vines.

Little thing that we don't forgive or forget can easily cause problems that will result in separations and/or divorce.

A few examples are;

You never say you love me anymore!

You don't greet me when I come home.

He leaves the toilet seat up.

You never listen to me.

You share your happiness, but not your hurts

Never spin quality time with me.

Never apologize

Making jokes of my shorts comings.

Fat jokes, short jokes, can't cook jokes, etc., etc.

Don't Let Satan Win Again

1st 6 six months of marriage honey is flowing

2nd 6 six months I'm tired, honey is going.

1st 6 months honey is dripping

2nd 6 months the devil is dipping

1st year: I feel you're present even when you are gone

2nd year: I am sometime lonely even when you are home

1st year: Into the marriage they can do no wrong

2nd year: it seems everything they do is wrong

1st year: I need you every minute of the day

2nd year: I need some time along please go away.

3rd year: We began taking the spouse for granted.

4th year: We are wondering if we made a mistake.

Satan laughs and rejoices when he sees your pain.

His four years of hard work has not been vain.

At this point the marriage becomes dysfunctional.

If there is no turnaround divorce is inevitable.

Satan wins again!

In any marriage there will be some good times and some hard times. If you cherish the good times, the reflection of those good times will help you get though the hard times.

Notes

Notes

Notes

Notes

Contact Information:

Bobby L. Woods

756 McTizic Street

Bolivar, TN 38008

call

731-658-9364 / 731-685-0017

or

email: tommie0713@att.net

ABOUT THE AUTHOR

Brother Bobby "Uncle Bob' Woods, a native Tennessean, raised on a farm near Whiteville, with six siblings. Our parents taught us the value of honesty and hard work.

My first experience with the Lord was at the age of eleven, at Bartlett Chapel Church. Because I did not understand about growing in the Lord, Satan stole what had been put in me. Therefore, I wasted precious time serving Satan. I was destroying my body with alcohol and cigarettes. But, thanks be to God for his Grace and Mercy that gave me another chance.

Every since that day, in Noon-day prayer, at Mt. Olivet Church of God in Christ in Dayton, Ohio, when God forgave me of my sins and filled me with the Holy Ghost, I've been trying to redeem the time. I endeavor to use every opportunity to let men, women, boys, and girls know that;

>**"God is Love,**
>
>**Jesus is Savior, the Holy Ghost is a Keeper"**

www.ingramcontent.com/pod-product-compliance
Lightning Source LLC
Chambersburg PA
CBHW071226090426
42736CB00014B/2991